More praise for *The Authentic C*

"An amazing method of giving form to feelings within the workplace."

— Joan Helpern, cofounder of Joan & David

"An insightful tool for those of us interested in experiencing our full potential and a more complete form of success."

— Christine Arena, author of
Cause for Success: Companies that Put Profits Second and Came in First

"Maggie Craddock's wonderful book *The Authentic Career* is part guidebook, part exploration of how to thoughtfully blend one's career path with the opportunity to self-actualize. Using real-life examples interspersed with her own wisdom and expertise, Craddock offers her readers a unique and striking method of finding one's own voice, balance, and satisfaction in the work world. A must read for anyone embarking on a new career or wishing to enhance their current work life."

— Susan Shapiro Barash,
author of *Reclaiming Ourselves* and *A Passion for More*

"A useful book for those struggling with career dissatisfaction. Read it if you feel you are giving more than you're getting."

— Nicholas Lore, author of *The Pathfinder: How to Choose or Change Your Career for a Lifetime of Satisfaction and Success*

THE
AUTHENTIC
CAREER

THE
AUTHENTIC
CAREER

Following the Path of Self-Discovery
to Professional Fulfillment

MAGGIE CRADDOCK

NEW WORLD LIBRARY
NOVATO, CALIFORNIA

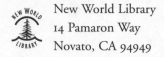

New World Library
14 Pamaron Way
Novato, CA 94949

Cover design by Mary Ann Casler
Interior design by Tona Pearce Myers

Library of Congress Cataloging-in-Publication Data
Craddock, Maggie.
  The authentic career : following the path of self-discovery to professional fulfillment / Maggie Craddock.
      p.   cm.
  ISBN 1-57731-438-7 (paper back : alk. paper)
1. Job satisfaction. 2. Job enrichment. 3. Career development.
4. Interpersonal relations. 5. Self-actualization (Psychology)
6. Professional employees—Conduct of life. 7. Success—Psychological aspects. I. Title.
  HF5549.5.J63C73 2004
  650.1—dc22   2003020865

First printing, February 2004
ISBN 1-57731-438-7
Printed in Canada on acid-free partially recycled paper
Distributed to the trade by Publishers Group West

10 9 8 7 6 5

To my mother and father,
Nancy and Perry,
who gave me the life, love, and support
that made all of this possible

Contents

This book has been inspired by the efforts of the many clients and colleagues whose search for personal and professional fulfillment has helped shape my coaching methodology. When their stories defied the conventional wisdom of how to overcome obstacles and achieve success, I learned to listen harder and question my own assumptions as well. Because I cannot list all of the courageous people I have had the privilege of working with, and because they all deserve recognition for the insights that have built this process, let me simply say that I thank each and every one of you for your support.

Acknowledgments

I'd like to thank Bobbi Mark, my agent, for her enthusiasm, tenacity, and friendship. She understood the tremendous need for this book from the beginning and has focused her substantial intellectual resources and dedication on getting it published. I'd also like to thank Linda Loewenthal, whose creative wisdom and professional insight has been invaluable in transforming this book from a dream into a reality.

Many thanks to my fabulous editor, Jason Gardner, who has made publishing this book a joyous experience. I'd also like to thank Mimi Kusch for her eagle eye and thoughtful insights on the editorial process.

Special thanks goes to Maria Nordone, who gave this work the kind of loving attention that can only come from a best friend. Maria's insights in the editing process came not only from her brilliant mind but also from her heart. Maria has stood by me every step of the way as I walked my own path toward authentic fulfillment. By sharing her life with me as only a true friend can, Maria has been my mirror of emotional and intellectual truth.

I'd also like to thank Judy Tobias Davis, who has become more than a friend as she has shared this journey with me — she has become family. Judy's fierce commitment to helping others and her tireless support of my efforts both personally and professionally has kept me going during many challenging periods as I was writing this book.

There are a few very special friends that must be mentioned individually because their presence in my life has been critical to the creation of this work. I'd like to thank Gwen Frey, whose spiritual integrity and healing wisdom has kept me focused. My very special thanks goes to Loreen Arbus, a friend and colleague who has taught me a new appreciation of the power that comes from the combination of professional commitment and a sincere desire to help others. Special thanks also to the dear friends and colleagues who have fed my spirit, warmed my heart, and encouraged my dreams: Debra Flanz, June Connors, Anne Vestal, Adrienne Hall, Lisa Vertucci, and Chloe Clark.

Special thanks goes to the members of the women's investment banking group at Credit Suisse First Boston. The professional integrity and commitment to excellence these women have shown as they worked through many of the principles in this book has been an inspiration to me.

As for the teachers throughout my journey, I'd like to thank the many special people who have touched my life from both Smith College and the London School of Economics. Over the years, both faculty and friends from these schools contributed to the educational foundation and the ongoing thirst for knowledge that helped me succeed on Wall Street and beyond. I'd also like to thank the many colleagues and friends I have made at both New York University's School of Social Work and the Ackerman Institute for the Family. Both of these organizations have been invaluable in helping me learn the science of counseling — and the art of helping human beings grow.

Many people tell me they would be delighted to work hard, take risks, and even make serious sacrifices to follow their life's dream — if only they knew what that dream was. As work demands more of our energy and time, people whose jobs hold little meaning beyond a paycheck find themselves suffering from poverty of purpose. Left unaddressed, this poverty eventually leads to professional sabotage.

One of the most dangerous types of professional sabotage takes place when, driven by a sense of panic that life is passing them by, people leave promising careers prematurely. The emotional drain of a career that seems to have no meaning becomes overwhelming. Without the patience or skills necessary to build the internal emotional foundation necessary for a successful career strategy, anyone can feel his or her job is a dead end, even when it isn't.

This book is for people struggling with job dissatisfaction. This process is equally helpful for people who are working to get to the next level in their current jobs as it is for people who are contemplating a career change. Whether your goal is to get promoted at your current firm, to launch a new career, or to decide what you want to do next, this process can help you. The Authentic Career Process is designed to help you get out of a professional rut, when you feel like you are giving more than you are getting, and to create a career that is an authentic reflection of your talents and desires.

This book began almost a decade ago on a trading floor. As a young portfolio manager at the investment firm Scudder, Stevens & Clark who had just won the Lipper Award for having the top-performing mutual fund in my fund class nationwide, I should have felt professionally fulfilled. What most people saw was a young woman who was quoted in the financial headlines, spoke frequently at national

Introduction

investment conferences, and had been profiled on a special segment of CNBC. What few people saw was someone who had worked with a variety of therapists to keep depression at bay and was spending virtually every weekend at a spiritual retreat trying to understand why success, an active social life, and tons of terribly expensive therapy weren't enough to help her feel whole.

For years I searched to find meaningful support in facing the challenges of protecting both my intellectual integrity and my intuition in a competitive corporate culture. Gradually, I learned that my situation was far from unique. What's more, in my search for meaningful answers, I found a direct parallel to what investors go through when searching for qualified money managers. Plenty of "experts" could outline the problems with what sounded like persuasive empathy, but few were actually able to deliver the solutions they proposed. What's more, many individuals trying to reconcile their powerfully competing drives for meaning and money become confused when they seek advice, since the disciplines of consulting, psychotherapy, and spiritual growth often remain jealously distinct.

This book offers you an executive coaching program that brings together some of the most valuable aspects of corporate consulting, psychoanalysis, and spiritual growth to guide you as you define and achieve success on your own terms. Please note that whenever I use the word *spiritual* in this book, I am referring to an individual's innate connection with his or her authentic nature — not to the ideology of any mainstream religious movement. Particularly today, when religion is being scrutinized for the same power struggles and philosophical confusion that plague our workplace cultures, if we don't separate the concepts of religion and spirituality, the viability of a spiritual perspective in helping us to overcome professional challenges will be seriously undermined.

In the business world, taking a "best practices" approach is using a strategic plan based on concepts that have proven effective in solving past critical problems. One of the most unique aspects of this approach

To believe your own thought, to believe that what is true for you in your private heart is true for all men — that is genius.

— Ralph Waldo Emerson

to coaching, as I will explain in this book, is its emphasis on the sequence that clients follow as they work through the ideas, feelings, behavior, and energy that form the building blocks of success. Following the proper sequence is vital to what I call the Authentic Career Process. Most of us consider the word *authentic* to mean the opposite of something that is false or fake. Initially, this may make the concept of an *authentic career* seem a bit ironic. After all, if you are collecting a paycheck, it's a real career, right? I use the term *authentic career,* however, to mean a truthful reflection of your genuine values and ideals as opposed to a reflection of the values and ideals of others.

This book also frequently asks you to make the distinction between the perspective of the "role" you have learned to play to survive and your "authentic self." For the purposes of this book, operating from your role means using the skills and traits you have developed over time to survive in your family and in your workplace. When the persona you use to survive forces you to compromise your values or your genuine desires, you are not behaving authentically.

In contrast, when you are operating from your authentic self you are functioning at the highest level you are capable of on your best day. As your authentic self evolves, your ability to function will improve, and your goals will be transformed as well. What's more, many of your less-than-ideal feelings and reactions are important aspects of the authentic self, since they are wakeup calls about things that need to be changed in your life. To be true to yourself, you need to embrace your less-than-perfect parts, or you will fall into the trap of behaving according to someone else's ideal of who you should be. The Authentic Career Process consists of four stages: the Awareness Stage, the Emotional Ownership Stage, the Interaction Stage, and the Integration Stage. Each stage is designed to help you achieve a series of goals that will lead to authentic success. The exercises you will complete in each stage provide the necessary insight and skill to successfully complete the work in the next stage.

An invasion of armies can be resisted, but not an idea whose time has come.

—Victor Hugo

STAGE I

AWARENESS

In the Awareness Stage, you will learn to separate what you really want in your life and career from what you have been taught by family, friends, and workplace cultures that you "should" want. This is a kind of mental sorting process. In a world where many of us have lost touch with our genuine desires because we've learned to base our self-esteem on others' approval, separating our ideas from those of others can be tricky indeed. The goals of the Awareness Stage are to:

How do geese know when to fly to the sun? Who tells them the seasons? How do we, humans, know when it is time to move on? As with the migrant birds, so surely with us, there is a voice within, if only we would listen to it, that tells us so certainly when to go forth into the unknown.

— Elisabeth Kübler-Ross

- Distinguish your personal values from the ideals you learned from your family and significant others

- Understand the role that financial considerations have played in your career choices

- Separate your desires from the goals dictated to you by others

People who are unable to separate their priorities and values from those of their bosses, their family, and the nonstop chatter of the media get caught in an internal civil war between what they truly want and what *others* have taught them they should want. Not only is this internal conflict draining, it also makes it virtually impossible to stay focused on goals long enough to take meaningful steps toward achieving them. The work in the Awareness Stage will help you to identify your authentic goals and separate them from others' agendas. This enhanced mental clarity provides the insight necessary to proceed to the next stage, Emotional Ownership.

STAGE II

EMOTIONAL OWNERSHIP

Challenging the limiting core beliefs identified in the Awareness Stage inevitably leads to an emotional backlash. Facing this backlash is a central part of the Emotional Ownership Stage. By strengthening your mind-body connection, you become better able to identify and release limiting emotions that would otherwise keep you paralyzed.

Enhancing this mind-body connection is vital to achieving success because taking meaningful risks creates powerful emotional responses. These responses don't just produce doubtful thoughts; they also induce physiological reactions, ranging from shallow breathing to a too-rapid heartbeat. What's more, you can't *think* your way through primal feelings such as fear. Like any feeling blocking our progress, fear lurks where we hide the things we don't want to know about ourselves. The work involved in the Emotional Ownership Stage helps you to release the energy devoted to avoiding these feelings and in the process clear out the emotional blocks holding you back. The goals of the Emotional Ownership Stage are to:

The privilege of a lifetime is being what you are.

— Joseph Campbell

- Identify the ways physical sensations stimulate thought patterns that "protect" you from what you would prefer not to know about yourself

- Understand the way the roles you have learned to play personally and professionally have helped you to suppress uncomfortable feelings

- Learn to channel the energy you had previously devoted to suppressing uncomfortable feelings into achieving your professional goals

Emotional energy is a source of tremendous power. To successfully focus your emotional energy, you must learn to trust your inner longings and the power of your imagination. Trusting your internal urges is a natural process that comes from heeding your body's signals and clearing the blocks restricting your range of emotional experience. The spontaneity you cultivate in this stage builds the self-trust necessary to put your ideas into action. This self-trust also gives you the courage necessary to proceed to the Interaction Stage.

He who does not lose his soul will endure.

— Lao-tzu

STAGE III

INTERACTION

The first half of the Authentic Career Process is largely introspective and stems from the premise that you can't be more successful than your self-image allows you to be. As you begin the Interaction Stage, you are at the midpoint of the coaching process. Here the emphasis shifts from an introspective focus to work that is interactive with the environment around you. The Interaction Stage is about translating your enhanced self-knowledge into effective action in the workplace.

Aerodynamically the bumble bee shouldn't be able to fly, but the bumble bee doesn't know it, and so goes on flying anyway.

— Mary Kay Ash

Your environment plays a powerful role in shaping your sense of self. Over time, the values, pace, and emotional tone of your work environment will subtly seep into your psyche. The way you are treated by your professional peers has a tremendous impact on your quality of life, both personally and professionally. When you walk down the halls of your office, what feelings are triggered? Is your workplace bustling with creativity and excitement? Is it saturated with tension and paranoia? In a world where more of us are working closer together, we end up sharing a lot more than a watercooler; we also share emotional highs and lows much more than we realize. The goals of the Interaction Stage are to:

- Help you understand the way your view of reality either resonates or clashes with the dominant values in your workplace

- Understand the importance of peer support and feedback in achieving your long-term career goals

- Monitor your internal responses to workplace challenges to develop options for transforming conflict into collaboration

Success is a team sport. The dominant beliefs and values of your workplace create a group energy that can either support or sabotage your career. To work harmoniously with the group energy of any workplace, you need to remember that the first place that energy is shifted is in the *self*. The behavioral skills you cultivate in the Interaction Stage will help you to develop the interpersonal relationships necessary to further your career. These professional alliances also form the foundation necessary for proceeding to the Integration Stage.

STAGE IV

INTEGRATION

The final stage of the Authentic Career Process helps you to explore the ways your sense of self, your emotional responses, and your significant relationships either can work together to reinforce your commitment to your life goals or can pull you in different directions and undermine your sense of purpose. The Integration Stage brings together the insights and skills you have developed throughout this process to help you focus every aspect of your being — your thoughts, your emotions, and even your spirit — on achieving your goals.

This stage is about practical spirituality. The work you do in this stage will help you to create a holistic definition of success — a success that is nourishing, not draining — that draws on your intellectual abilities and your intuition simultaneously. While we all experience flashes of intuition, this work is designed to help you cultivate the ability to trust your inner knowing consistently rather than erratically. The goals of the Integration Stage are to:

- Harmonize your private desires with your public goals

- Cultivate enough mental flexibility for your intuition and intelligence to reinforce each other

- Unify your need for recognition with your desire to help others

The professional creativity this work unleashes is increasingly critical in a business climate where we are called on to grasp all sides of difficult questions — not just the sides we are emotionally comfortable with. When we are in touch with our inner knowing, we remember that an infinite number of solutions exist to any professional challenge. By working through the fears that lock us into the limited perspective

All intelligent thoughts have already been thought; what is necessary is only to try to think them again.

— Goethe

of a restrictive workplace or family system, we become free to achieve our full professional potential.

The following is a brief synopsis of my personal journey through the Authentic Career Process to show how these four stages have shaped my life as well as my coaching methodology.

MY STORY

In 1992, when I had just entered my thirties as a portfolio manager, my success propelled me onto CNBC and into the financial pages of newspapers across the country. From the outside, it looked like I had it all — a great apartment, great clothes, plenty of money in the bank, and an active dating life. From the inside, things were a little less pristine.

To put my cycle into perspective, let me backtrack a bit to 1987 when I was counting the change in my wallet to figure out how my two housemates and I were going to eat over the weekend. Suddenly, the phone rang. It was one of the big-time investors a family friend had introduced me to at his private club. (My life in those days involved wild economic swings between lavish restaurants and Campbell's soup on the fire escape.) He wanted to know how my job hunt was going. "Still looking," I sighed. "Thanks for asking. How are you?" There was a long silence. Then he replied quietly, "I lost $60 million today."

Welcome to the terrifying job market of 1987. Within four months of graduating from the London School of Economics I was facing one of the largest stock market crashes in American history. It was also one of the toughest years to find a job in financial services.

Never believe you can't find a job in the worst of times. Three years of dogged persistence later, I had managed to carve out a career as a global bond analyst at Alliance Capital. I loved getting to the trading floor at 6 A.M. Every day, the story of the world played out across the international currency markets like a giant novel unfolding a new chapter. I kept meticulous notes on changes in interest rate spreads around the world and on global economic fundamentals with the love

The genius is in the details.

— Ansel Adams

of a cloistered monk driven by the satisfaction of getting every pen stroke right. In my desk drawer, I also kept a detailed paper-trading journal of all my investment recommendations and never told my colleagues about my growing aspirations.

Over time, as my paper-trading journal managed to hold its own against the bets of the "big boys," my aspirations hardened into ambition. I found myself in the grip of a full-fledged drive to become a portfolio manager myself. On the face of it, this aspiration seemed hopelessly deluded. My boss was busily hiring boisterous young men who, in my opinion, seemed more focused on self-promotion than on learning the art of investing. But he was teaching these guys the trading skills they needed to actually participate in the market, while I was stuck being the administrative assistant who crunched the numbers and printed the charts.

Time passed, and the increasing sophistication of my research became closely correlated with my boss's general irritation with me. By this time, I was writing a weekly statistical report on macroeconomic developments in the various international bond markets we covered. At one point, one of the portfolio managers in the firm liked my work enough to send copies to the board of directors of one of the firm's Fortune 500 clients. "Who does she think she *is?*" thundered my boss in rage when he heard. At this point it dawned on me that this guy wasn't exactly poised to nurture my professional development. I figured I had two choices: I could stay huddled in my cubicle and try to spike his coffee with Prozac, or I could look for another job. I opted for the latter.

By 1993 I was standing on the balcony at a spectacular resort in Laguna Beach during an internal investment conference. I had become a portfolio manager at Scudder, Stevens & Clark, and in the previous year my team had won the Lipper Award for the best-performing short-term global bond and currency fund in the nation.

As I surveyed the idyllic setting around me, I realized that I felt completely empty inside. Noticing that this emotional black hole had grown large enough to eclipse these natural wonders surrounding me

Being defeated is often a temporary condition. Giving up is what makes it permanent.

— Marlene vos Savant

was my first hint that something was very, very wrong. Around this time, two professional experiences came together to light a spark that eventually was to blaze into a complete change of career. First, I was exposed to some outside consultants and behavioral experts whom management had retained to help us stay competitive under pressure. Second, I was coached for interviews with SEC representatives who were trying to keep up with investment innovations. Separately, neither encounter might have particularly affected me. Together, they changed my life.

The consultants and behavioral experts — we hadn't yet heard the term *executive coach* in those days — who came to help us had their work cut out for them. Most people who worked on a trading floor attended these seminars on topics ranging from diversity to client service at gunpoint. We were there to make money, and anything that took us away from our jobs left us cranky at best and on a bad day hostile. We sat around conference tables, adopted polite masks of resignation, and suppressed inner screams of frustration when these "human resource types" suggested that we all go around the table and introduce ourselves. The relaxed pace was an agonizing contrast to the hyped-up internal pace at which we led our lives. Since senior management was paying the bills, many of us feared these well-intentioned outsiders would never get to the real problems.

Meanwhile, the SEC interviews presented us with another group of outsiders struggling to understand our work from a different angle. I remember answering one regulatory representative's questions as honestly and clearly as possible but at the same time thinking to myself, "I know the information you're after, but you don't know the best way to phrase your question to get at it." It was a moment of epiphany. If I knew where that particular SEC guy was today, I'd give him a hug. "That's what's holding our consultants back!" it dawned on me. "They haven't worked in a place like this long enough to internalize the culture, so they don't know how to frame their questions to get at the real problems!" It was in that moment of insight that my professional transition began.

Liberty means responsibility. That is why most men dread it.

— George Bernard Shaw

Long before I had ever heard the words *executive* and *coach* put together in the same sentence, I realized that there was a need for individuals who could help people at all levels of professional development balance the overlapping economic and emotional challenges they faced in a rapidly changing economy. To become the helping professional I desperately needed at one point in my career but could not find, I researched various counseling degrees and pursued the one I felt was best suited to providing emotional support in a corporate environment. I chose social work.

I've dedicated myself to this work, because not only is this a process I've developed to empower others; it is also a process I have lived. My Awareness Stage took place during my years as a portfolio manager. As I dealt with both market challenges and clients' fears during a variety of market cycles, I had a realization. When my trading team and I were buying and selling securities, what we were really doing was dealing in peace of mind.

As I became more aware of the core beliefs and desires driving the portfolio-management industry, I also became aware that the most important investment of my life was my investment in myself. The more I realized this, the more my airplane reading switched from investment research to books on personal growth. During my last two years in financial services, my ambitions changed from the specialized work of helping people create profitable portfolios to the broader work of helping people create profitable lives.

Adventure is worthwhile in itself.

—Amelia Earhart

The decision to forge a new career helping people invest in themselves was only the starting point. My Emotional Ownership work involved digging deep into myself and finding the courage to put my beliefs into practice at a time when there was no discipline known as executive coaching. I was acting on the faith that helping people listen to their inner voice would not only make it possible for them to identify what they wanted to do, it would also help them find a way to get paid to do it. The emotional backlash that I struggled with as this dream formed inside of me involved wrestling with inner doubts that threatened to paralyze me. In those days, the industries of consulting, psychotherapy, and spiritual growth were well established but often poorly integrated. How dare I, as a beginner, attempt to cross boundaries in multiple disciplines simultaneously?

Once I started to take action, the years that I spent developing the inner resilience to follow my dream were critical to my success. My Interaction Stage began as I researched a variety of academic programs to get the therapeutic training I knew I needed to deal responsibly with the issues that come up in coaching. For example, helping people evaluate the risks of taking professional steps such as leaving a corporate career and working as an entrepreneur almost always brought up related emotional challenges. A client's spouse might have strong feelings about a change in the family's cash flow, and he or she might have to battle anxiety and even mild depression during the initial stages of living with an uncertain income.

Researching various psychoanalytic and spiritual approaches for dealing with people's personal reactions to life-changing events brought me into contact with many people who have been enthusiastic supporters of my efforts. However, there were just as many "experts" who sought to discourage my efforts when they threatened the boundaries of previously established methodologies. The inner resolve that I had cultivated in the first two stages of my own Authentic Career Process gave me the courage I needed to negotiate with and learn from others when my convictions were on the line. Over time, staying true to my inner beliefs enabled me to be teachable while remaining true to myself.

My work in the Integration Stage is an ongoing process. My coaching career has brought me into contact with people who teach me new things every day. However, my evolution as a coach is an example of the principle that every success brings with it the seeds of new challenges. Even though I have the privilege of working with clients in a variety of industries around the world, to do this work effectively I must strive to keep my own inner world quiet enough to remain receptive, to listen for what people cannot give themselves permission to say, and to

Far away there in the sunshine are my highest aspirations. I may not reach them, but I can look up and see their beauty, believe in them, and try to follow where they lead.

— Louisa May Alcott

maintain hope. This process involves fighting for quiet time in my life and remembering to nurture my humanity as well as my professional growth.

The energy of success is created *between* people, not just as a result of their individual abilities. My hope for everyone who works through this process is not only that you achieve the success you desire but also that you build relationships along the way that prove to be equally rewarding.

Not truth, but faith,
it is that keeps
the world alive.

— Edna St. Vincent Millay

BEFORE YOU GET STARTED

This book is divided into four parts, or stages. Each stage is divided into three chapters containing exercises integral to building the skills and understanding necessary for the next stage of the process. In turn each exercise gives you some background on how the exercise relates to the overall process, instructions for doing the exercise, and an example of a selected client's experience doing this exercise. Following each vignette of a selected client's experience are some general reflections on what you may experience as you complete this part of the process.

I built the Authentic Career Process on this series of exercises, some of which may bring up some fairly strong emotions as you work through them, because I believe that we attain self-knowledge through emotional realizations. Intellectual concepts that are not reinforced by the emotional energy of personal experience can provide us with entertainment, hope, and inspiration — but they are unlikely to foster meaningful changes in our lives.

I recommend that you keep a journal or notebook as you proceed through the exercises, since you will need to refer to your answers from some of the earlier exercises when completing the later ones. You may choose to work through each exercise in depth as you go through the book. Alternatively, you may decide to read through a particular stage of the process or even the entire book before attempting the exercises. Follow your own internal guidance in how to get started. If you don't have the time to complete every exercise, I suggest that you read through the goals in each chapter and focus on those exercises associated with the goal where you feel you need the most work.

I have changed the names and some defining details in all the client examples to protect confidentiality. However, while the names are fictitious, the situations are not. The stories I tell about the challenges these individuals are dealing with and the experiences they have had as they go through this process are all true.

Here are some additional suggestions for getting the most out of this book:

- *Take your time.* One of the most personal parts of the Authentic Career Process is discovering the most effective pace for you. Some people are in a hurry when it comes to doing anything to further their professional ambitions. If you find yourself rushing, remember that often it doesn't take much longer to do this work thoughtfully than it does to do it superficially. If you find yourself wondering if you are moving too quickly in some stages, be sure to take some time to reflect on the work you have done in previous exercises. This will keep you in tune with the sequence of your progress. Other people may face the opposite challenge; they may find that they move so slowly when immersed in personal material that they risk losing sight of how their progress in one part of the process is related to the rest of it. Since you are working with some powerful concepts, trust yourself if it feels right to take a breather for a few days. However, don't pause for too long, since it is important to keep a sense of how you are progressing sequentially to get the most powerful results.

- *Be gentle with yourself as you approach these exercises.* Pushing yourself to complete an entire chapter on a long plane flight may be possible — but it's not necessarily advisable. Remember, trying too hard can be a form of resistance.

- *Set the mood.* The goal of this work is to bring your entire being into the change process so that you can take meaningful action to

I've been dreaming, looking, for as far back as I had any thought of what it should be like to be a human being. My desire was to be free as soon as I had learned that there had been slavery of human beings and that I was a descendant from them.

— Rosa Parks

live the life of your dreams — and not just live "virtually" in your mind where your goals are ideas rather than realities. Focusing our entire being means taking into account that all our senses are important when it comes to concentrating and unblocking our energy. For centuries spiritual schools, both Eastern and Western, have taught that it is the "primitive" part of the mind that is the gateway to the "chi," or life-force energy. The primitive part of us is related to our earliest ancestry — our animal senses. Calming the senses to focus the energy of the primal part of our being is the purpose of the soothing scenery of Zen gardens, the chanting of the Native Americans, the incense used in Catholic rites, and so on. Since we've known for centuries the power of stimulating our senses in conjunction with our minds, why not use this insight to achieve your professional goals? Put on some background music that helps set the right mood, and keep some snacks on hand. Focusing on doing these exercises meaningfully takes energy!

Never mistake knowledge for wisdom.
One helps you make a living; the other helps you make a life.
— Sandra Carey

- *Remember to take breaks.* There are no shortcuts to finding authentic personal power. Doing part of an exercise with clarity is better than forcing yourself to complete the entire thing half-heartedly.

- *Remember that there's no right way to do this work; just be true to yourself.* There are an infinite number of ways to succeed using the insights and tools that this process will help you develop. It's fascinating to see the difference between the way my corporate clients and my clients who are professional artists approach these exercises — particularly in the initial stages of the process. The corporate clients will often email their completed exercises in advance and come in with carefully phrased and spell-checked responses that read like executive summaries. In contrast, the actors and artists I have worked with will come in with dog-eared worksheets studded with colorful Post-it notes and responses that often sound like poetry. There's no right or wrong way. The way you do this work is a reflection of the way you live. Note that this also applies to whether you do the work at all!

- *Take some time to reflect on your work a few days after you have done a particular exercise.* Putting the work down for a few days and reviewing it later will allow the emotions and insights that this work elicits to incubate at the less-conscious level of your mind.

Power is the ability to get things done.

— Rosabeth Moss Kanter

The exercises in *The Authentic Career* can be powerful transformative tools for your career and your life — provided you approach them with the right attitude. The level of commitment with which you do these exercises will determine whether they provide you with some temporary diversion or a life-changing insight.

Many people have told me that they have gotten tremendous benefits simply from reading this book. However, it is the people who take the time to actually do the exercises who report the most life-changing results. Time is precious to us all. My wish for all of you is that you grant yourself the gift of time you need to deepen your relationship with your authentic self. This investment cannot help but bring you closer to achieving your dreams.

STAGE I
AWARENESS

The Awareness Stage is about learning the difference between what you truly want from your career and what you have been taught you "should" want by your family, your friends, and other important people in your life.

Most people are eager for a quick fix. Let me rephrase: most people are desperate for a quick fix. By the time they come to coaching, many people have been dealing with career frustrations for so long that they want things to improve immediately. However, often a key part of their problem is that they are confused about what they really want from their careers. To be successful, you must be honest with yourself about what you truly want. To establish a firm foundation for your career strategy, or for any type of personal growth, you must distinguish between the goals that reflect your genuine desires and those that reflect what other people think you should do.

For the caged bird sings of freedom.

— Maya Angelou

Going through life being who other people want us to be eventually hurts us. People who have mastered the art of morphing into whatever their clients and managers want them to be to get ahead often tell me, "I'd happily take half my current salary if I could find a job where I could truly be myself." Many of these top performers secretly struggle with depression and mood swings. This is because, over time, suppressing one's individuality begins to take its toll.

The Awareness Stage provides you with a foundation for building a personal career strategy that does not require you to suppress vital aspects of your individuality to achieve your goals. The work in this first stage is divided into three chapters:

- *Chapter 1: "Your Mental Detective Work."* The first chapter of the Awareness Stage is devoted to clarifying what "success" means to you based on the core beliefs about work and life you have internalized from your family. We have all scripted a personal story for ourselves based on how we expect — or hope — our lives and careers will unfold. The Awareness Stage begins by helping you develop some objectivity in assessing the way that your family's values have influenced your professional priorities.

- *Chapter 2: "Your Monetary Detective Work."* The second chapter focuses on clarifying the role that your thoughts about personal wealth play in your career decisions. It is vital to determine how much of your professional focus is driven by financial considerations and how much is driven by other concerns about the quality of your life. For example, your ability to tolerate the risk of an uncertain income stream can powerfully influence the type of career you pursue. Likewise, the amount of money you need to feel secure may influence the professional options that seem meaningful to you.

- *Chapter 3: "The Mental Alchemy of Releasing the 'Shoulds.'"* By the time you reach the final chapter of the Awareness Stage, you will be more conscious of the ways your personal history and your core beliefs about success and financial security have influenced your career choices. This background information is a prerequisite for clarifying the difference between your genuine desires and the goals you have decided to pursue based on others' values. The exercises in this chapter are designed to help you identify the beliefs that have been limiting your career choices and to help you focus on your authentic priorities.

The question "what shall we do?" is the wrong question. The question is then, "How shall we be?"

— Sonia Johnson

CHAPTER 1

Your Mental Detective Work

The first thing that anyone beginning this process needs to confront is where his or her story is breaking down. Thus, the first goal of the Awareness Stage is to help you clarify which of your family's ideas about success you have internalized. Each of us nurtures a dream of our professional prospects — and the scope of this dream is often dictated by our history.

Many people would agree that having a great career is one of the most important aspects of their lives. What's more, many confess that when their professional progress seems blocked, they often spend endless hours strategizing and worrying about how to improve the situation. However, regardless of the amount of time they have spent pondering their progress, many people who begin coaching are surprised to learn how fuzzy their thought process has been about why they are doing what they are doing professionally.

My first meeting with Stanley illustrates this point. Stanley is a young man who has been working in banking for the past two years. I began by asking what prompted him to seek coaching at this point in his career. Stanley responded with a succession of the kind of war stories that have become all too familiar to me.

"I don't trust my boss, and I don't respect him," Stanley began angrily. "I have my annual review next week (a typical first-session cliff-hanger), and my top priority with you today is to figure out how to make the most of this meeting and keep from getting fired. I'm sure he's reviewed me poorly because I can barely get through a day without him asking me a bunch of demeaning questions about how many meetings I have scheduled for the week and how early I am getting in each morning. It's demoralizing to be scrutinized like this. I'm a vice president, not a truant schoolchild — how dare he!"

Obviously, Stanley was experiencing extreme frustration because his relationship with his boss was not supporting his story. Our work in the initial part of the Awareness Stage was designed to provide Stanley with a deeper understanding in two key areas. First, he needed to be as clear as possible about what his long-term professional aspirations were (many people who begin coaching are amazed to discover that these are far more vague than they had thought). Second, he needed a more objective view of the cycle of behavioral interaction that was going on between him and his boss and how this cycle was feeding the growing tension between them.

"How does your current job fit into your long-term strategy for building the right career for you?" I asked him.

He was thoughtful for a moment. Obviously, this was not the type of question he had stopped to ponder before our session. "I'm not sure," he started cautiously, as if it were a trick question or a test he could fail in some way. "I've always wanted to be in finance . . . I mean, it pays a decent salary, and I work with lots of smart people."

"Well, why banking?" I pressed gently. "I mean, there are lots of ways to make a living in financial services. What makes this position particularly appealing to you?"

"Well . . . it's just the first company I joined after graduating. I took a job as an incoming associate, and I went where they put me. Now I'm in a department where I have at least some experience, so if I want to get ahead I figure I'd better put my head down and make this job work."

"Are there any other jobs at your firm that you think you might enjoy more?" I continued. "I mean, you must interface with other departments in the course of getting information for your clients."

"Well, sometimes," he ventured, "but it's not even practical to discuss this. There is no way that my firm is going to let me change jobs just because I think I'd prefer working in another department. That's ridiculous!"

"Why is that ridiculous?" I asked.

Nothing is a stronger influence psychologically on their environment, and especially on their children, than the unlived lives of the parents.

— Carl Jung

"Because they don't care about me and my career," he responded angrily. "All they care about is money!"

"Not even if your understanding of a certain aspect of the business means that your efforts there could be profitable to them?" I queried.

"Not even then," he countered defensively.

"So, let me be sure I understand what you are telling me. You are saying that you are working at a job that you aren't sure you like, for a boss you are pretty convinced you don't like, at a firm that you are confident doesn't care about you. Am I understanding your position clearly?" I asked him.

"Well, it sounds pretty grim when you put it all together that way," he said thoughtfully, "but to be honest with you, I think you've pretty much got the picture."

"Why are you doing this?" I asked him. "It certainly doesn't sound like much fun."

"It's not," he responded sadly. "But I'm determined to make enough money so that my wife can retire and stay home with our kids in a couple of years if she wants to. It's also important to me to be part of a respected organization so that I feel like a professional. It may sound silly, but I've worked so hard getting through school and into a firm like this that I'll feel like a failure if I can't make it work."

"You mentioned that being part of a respected organization makes you feel like a professional. What does this mean to you specifically?"

"Well, it means working with a group that I feel proud to associate myself with and making enough money to support a family. The fact of the matter is that I haven't thought much about that, specifically, and while I guess that's sort of lame, I don't think many of the people I work with have thought about this stuff either. I just want to earn a nice salary and get ahead. Is that so bad?" he asked.

"Not at all," I reassured him. "Just as long as you have some definition of getting ahead that's meaningful for you."

"I guess I'm a little stumped on that one," he replied.

"Then that's where we'll begin."

Most people who come to me are in the process of starting to explore their real potential. Many of us have been so busy living up to the expectations of others that we have lost touch with our authentic sense of self. The ability to separate our values and perceptions from those of our bosses, our family members, and the nonstop chatter of the media to indulge in the luxury of independent thought requires time for personal reflection, which seems to be getting harder and harder to come by.

Moreover, many people who become discouraged about their professional prospects spend much of their energy contemplating whether or not to leave their jobs. Understanding the way your background influences your perspective on your career is vital to preventing the professional sabotage that takes place when an individual leaves his or her job prematurely because of short-term frustration. However, this insight is equally important in helping you face the facts when you find that you must leave a job because it is unfulfilling or it forces you to compromise your values.

The first exercise in the Awareness Stage is designed to help you do the mental detective work necessary to clarify the values and beliefs that have shaped your career choices over time. This exercise systematically explores your memories of the people and experiences that have significantly influenced your ideas about professional success.

We are the heroes of our own story.

— Mary McCarthy

Children begin by loving their parents; as they grow older they judge them; sometimes they forgive them.

— Oscar Wilde

EXERCISE:

YOUR PERSONAL TREE OF LIFE

You begin this exercise by reflecting on an assortment of family pictures. I use photos in many of my coaching exercises because these personal images often help us to access all sorts of information from our subconscious. I suggest lugging out the whole album or packing a selection of photos in a portable album if you are going to do this exercise while traveling. You are going to use these pictures as a catalyst for asking some powerful questions aimed at getting to the heart of your beliefs about work and about how much money you believe you need to feel successful.

This exercise was designed to uncover some powerful formative beliefs as efficiently as possible. I've needed to adopt a variety of methods for examining these belief systems with clients who desperately need perspective in this area but are frequently firmly committed to avoiding this. Some coaching clients who are sent to me by their firm's human resources department begin the process convinced that everyone else is riddled with problems — while they are blameless and tragically misunderstood. "I don't have time for this therapeutic bullshit," I've had clients thunder in protest. "I've been in therapy before, and it didn't do any darned good. I'm not going over all that personal stuff again . . . it's just exhausting."

*What was silent
in the father speaks in the
son, and often I found in
the son the unveiled
secret of the father.*

— Friedrich Nietzsche

Part of what makes the Personal Tree of Life exercise work is that it involves answering detailed questions about your family that might not occur to you on your own. These questions deal with family secrets and areas that many people initially avoid scrutinizing. You don't have to be a die-hard Freudian to acknowledge that family is the first and greatest influence in your life. If you want to know what a woman thinks about men, look at the men in her life, beginning with her father. The men who surround a particular woman and with whom she has chosen to interact reflect what being "male" means to her. Similarly, if you want to know what a man thinks about women, first look at his mother; then look at the women he surrounds himself with both personally and professionally. Many psychologists even assert that one's father forms the foundation for his or her concept of "God the father." (If you're a reader with children, no pressure, huh?) This early molding is particularly powerful when it comes to the emotionally loaded concepts of success and financial security.

We all internalize a sense of what the significant people in our lives mean to us. These internalizations gradually become the inner voices that influence us in prioritizing all the vast stimuli bombarding our consciousness so that we can assign meaning to an event, integrate this meaning into our overall perception of reality, and then decide on a course of action. This lively neurological circus is going on in the recesses of your mind when you say "good morning" to the boss in the hall and he sullenly ignores you. "I wonder if he thinks I'm not important enough to acknowledge?" can be one of the theories that start firing as your mind seeks to assign meaning to this disheartening event. "I'll never get ahead in this place" may flash across your consciousness as the perception of reality darkens. Such a train of thought may lead a disheartened employee to try even harder to please, go home early in a huff, or even update his or her résumé — it all depends on how he or she has been conditioned to respond to rejection. This conditioning starts in the family.

You'll need a selection of family photos, including parents, grandparents, and as many extended relatives as you can think of — group shots from family reunions are great for this. You'll also need a journal, a pad of paper, or a laptop to enter your answers to the questions in this exercise. If your photos are loose or detachable from your album, begin by spreading them out in front of you in three rows based on different generations of your family. If they are glued into an album and won't budge, draw three rows on a piece of paper and make note of the names of various family members in these rows where you would place their pictures if the photos were detachable.

The middle row should have your mother on the left hand side and your dad on the right. The top row should consist of your grandparent's generation, with your mother's parents and your aunts and uncles on her side on the left and your father's parents and his extended family generally on the right. This system isn't going to be perfect, of course, because group shots are going to have multiple generations in them — but if you just get things generally positioned, you will be doing fine. Finally, the bottom row should be made up of you, your spouse or significant other if you have one, your kids, your siblings, and all your nieces and nephews.

We are going to start this exercise in the middle row by reflecting

When you teach your son, you teach your son's son.

— The Talmud

on your parents. If, by the way, your birth parents are divorced and you were primarily raised by a stepparent, then feel free to work with your thoughts concerning this individual. You should adjust these questions in any way necessary to reflect the specifics of your family situation. When I do this exercise with clients, I'm constantly encountering variations on the traditional family tree, and I'm used to helping people who only have partial information about the names, ages, and even the existence of some of their relatives. Please follow your heart and use your common sense in working with the information you have in the way that is most meaningful for you. The purpose of this exercise is to gain an enhanced awareness of your fundamental belief system and how it has been formed — not to be genealogically precise.

Take your time. It is better to do this exercise thoughtfully than to rush through it.

You are welcome to start with either parent, but for the purpose of illustration I have arbitrarily chosen to start with your mother.

REFLECTING ON YOUR MOTHER

The laws governing the universe can be made interesting and wonderful to children . . . and they begin to ask: What am I? What is the task of humanity in this wonderful universe?

— **Maria Montessori**

Begin by selecting a picture of your mother that resonates with you, and then jot down a few descriptive words of what comes to mind. For example, you may find yourself jotting down anything from "loving, caring, and nurturing" to "sad, controlling, and vulnerable." There are no right or wrong words; this is about your emotional truth, and no one else has to agree with it. Try not to edit your thought process. Your goal in this exercise is simply to do some good mental detective work.

Once you have an initial impression of what "mom" means to you, I'd like you to answer the following questions. Take your time with them. Try to get an internal sense of how your mother would answer these questions if she were there in the room with you. If any pictures of your mother in specific situations pop into your head as you reflect on these images and jot down some notes about this. Sometimes these pictures give us clues about our deeper thought process much more efficiently than words do.

1. Did your mother ever work outside the home?
2. Was your mother successful in the eyes of her community? Was she successful in her own eyes?
3. If so, how did she feel about her work? If not, how did she feel about being a homemaker?
4. How did your mother's working role influence her sense of self?
5. What were your mother's attitudes about money? How did she handle money?
6. Did your mother feel that your family was financially comfortable when you were growing up, or was she anxious about finances?
7. How did your mother's relationship with money affect her quality of life?
8. What values did your mother instill in you concerning money?
9. What were your mother's dreams for you of the role that work would play in your life?

Each of us brings to our job, whatever it is, our lifetime of experience and our values.

— Sandra Day O'Connor

REFLECTING ON YOUR FATHER

Now find a picture of your father that resonates with you and start by writing down the first words that pop into your head. Again, try to be as spontaneous and nonjudgmental as possible.

When you have recorded your initial impression of "dad," take a stab at the following questions:

1. What did your father do for a living?
2. Was your father successful in the eyes of his community? Was he successful in his own eyes?
3. How did your father's career influence his sense of self?
4. Did your father ever struggle with periods of unemployment?
5. What were your father's attitudes about money? How did he handle money?

6. Did your father feel that your family was financially comfortable when you were growing up, or was he anxious about finances?

7. How did your father's relationship with money affect his quality of life?

8. What values did your father instill in you concerning money?

9. What were his dreams for you of the role that work would play in your life?

THE BOND BETWEEN YOUR PARENTS

Now we are going to consider the impact your mom and dad's feelings about professional fulfillment and personal wealth had on their relationship. Keeping their relationship in mind, answer the following questions:

1. What was the power balance between your mother and father? When there was conflict, was one of them more likely to be the victor? If so, which one, and why?

2. Was the power balance in your home affected by your parents' professional and personal responsibilities? If so, how?

3. Did your parents' respective levels of personal wealth or attitudes about money have an impact on the power balance in your home? If so, how?

4. What are the similarities and differences between your parents in terms of how they defined work and success?

5. What are the similarities and differences between your parents in terms of how they felt about how much money it takes to be financially secure?

6. Which parent has had the most influence on your attitudes toward spending and saving? Why?

7. Which parent has most powerfully influenced your professional decisions, and why? (Hint: Even if your career is heading in the opposite direction from what you believe a particular parent would have chosen for you, this parent may have still exerted an extremely powerful influence on your decisions.)

8. If your parents are living, how do they feel about your current job and your level of financial security? If they are deceased, how do you think they would feel about your current circumstances?

TAKING IT UP A GENERATION: YOUR MOTHER'S FAMILY

Now it's time to go up a generation and consider the ways your maternal grandparents may have shaped your mother's views about work and financial security. Take a minute to reflect on the photos of your maternal grandparents (or on your memories of them if no photos are available). Jot down the first descriptive words that come to mind when you think of them. You are going to take a deeper look at the circumstances that may have contributed to your mother's core beliefs about financial security and wealth. With this goal in mind, answer the following questions:

1. Did your maternal grandmother have a job outside the home? How did her life's work, either as a homemaker or in some other capacity, influence her sense of self and her satisfaction with her life?

2. What did your maternal grandfather do for a living? Was he successful in the eyes of his community? In his own eyes?

3. How many brothers and sisters did your mother have growing up? Where was she in the birth order?

4. Did your mother come from a wealthy family? If so, what impact did this have on the emotional dynamics in your mother's family?

5. Did your mother's family have enough money when your mother was a child, or was financial survival a struggle?

6. What were the respective attitudes of your maternal grandmother and grandfather about saving and spending?

7. Which one of your mother's parents do you think had the most powerful impact on the way she saw her purpose in life and defined success?

8. How did the financial circumstances of your mother's family influence the emotional tone of your mother's childhood?

What are a family's "rules" regarding interaction with outside systems and media? This is an increasingly important issue today as the media reaches into our bedrooms at night and our cell phones remain on twenty-four hours a day.

— Evan Imber-Black

TAKING IT UP A GENERATION: YOUR FATHER'S FAMILY

Now I'd like you to go through the same exercise with your paternal grandparents. Focusing on the way your dad's childhood circumstances may have contributed to his core beliefs about success and financial security, answer the following questions:

1. Did your paternal grandmother have a job outside the home? How did her life's work, either as a homemaker or in some other capacity, influence her sense of self and her satisfaction with her life?

2. What did your paternal grandfather do for a living? Was he successful in the eyes of his community? In his own eyes?

3. How many brothers and sisters did your father have growing up? Where was he in the birth order?

4. Did your father come from a wealthy family? If so, what impact did this have on the emotional dynamics in your father's family?

5. Did your father's family have enough money when your father was a child, or was financial survival a struggle?

6. What were the respective attitudes of your paternal grandmother and grandfather about saving and spending?

7. Which one of your father's parents do you think had the most powerful impact on the way he saw his purpose in life and defined success?

8. How did the financial circumstances of your father's family influence the emotional tone of your father's childhood?

The first idea that a child must acquire in order to be actively disciplined is that of the difference between good and evil; and the task of educators lies in seeing that a child does not confound good with immobility, and evil with activity.

— Maria Montessori

REFLECTIONS ON YOUR GENERATION

(If you are an only child, skip this section.)

Now we will review the ways your family "belief matrix" may have affected your perceptions of professional fulfillment and personal wealth. What I mean by a belief matrix is the mutually reinforcing set of core beliefs and values that characterizes the way that your family has interacted with the world.

Consider where you are in the birth order. Starting with your eldest sibling, jot down the first descriptive words that come to mind when you think of this brother or sister. Keep going down the line in chronological order and make some brief reflective notes on all your siblings. When you have finished, answer the following questions:

1. How do your siblings' attitudes toward work and professional fulfillment reflect your parents' values? How do they differ?

2. Which of your siblings is considered the most professionally successful by your family, and why? (Feel free to indicate yourself if that seems the appropriate response to this or any other question.)

3. How does the family's attitude toward this sibling's success affect his or her sense of self and quality of life?

4. How do your siblings' attitudes toward wealth and financial security reflect your parents' values? How do they differ?

5. Which of your siblings is the wealthiest, and how does this influence his or her standing in the family? (Reflect on how this influences you if appropriate.)

6. How does this sibling's wealth affect his or her sense of self and quality of life?

7. If your siblings are married with children, how are your family's attitudes toward success and financial security reflected in the next generation through the children? How do you feel about this?

8. How successful are you considered in your family relative to your siblings? How does this affect your sense of self and what you believe you are capable of professionally?

One faces the future with one's past.

— Pearl S. Buck

Stories determine real effects in terms of shaping people's lives.

— Michael White

THE IMPACT OF YOUR SIGNIFICANT OTHER

The following questions will help you consider the role of your spouse or significant other in shaping your attitudes toward success and financial security. Even if you are single at the moment, you may want to answer the following questions by reflecting on past partners or on how you would feel about an ideal mate. Reflect on a picture of your significant other, and jot down the first descriptive words that come into your mind. After making some reflective notes, answer the following questions:

1. Has your partner been a significant part of your life for some time, or is he or she a new addition to your inner circle?
2. How does the length of time you have been with this person affect the amount of influence that he or she has in shaping your beliefs?
3. How does your partner's career choice influence the dynamic between the two of you?
4. How does your partner define success, and does he or she feel professionally fulfilled?
5. Do your respective financial situations and levels of earning power have an impact on the power balance in your relationship? If so, how? If not, why not?
6. If you have children, how are you and your partner communicating your values about success and personal wealth to them?
7. If you have children, what beliefs about the meaning of work and the value of money do you see your children exhibiting? How does this affect your sense of self as a parent?

If you have worked through this process sincerely, most likely it has been rather intense for you. It is critical that, upon completing this exercise, you spend some reflective time alone allowing your thoughts to settle. Honoring the time you need to process your thoughts and feelings reinforces your self-respect. Perhaps you unwind in the bathtub, or by going running. If it's late at night, you may want to allow yourself to meditate quietly before you go to sleep. Whatever you choose to do, it is critical that you spend some quiet time integrating the thoughts and feelings that you have been sifting through without forcing yourself to do anything that feels like "work."

To help give you a fuller understanding of this work and what you may experience by doing it, now let's consider Stanley's experience doing the Personal Tree of Life exercise.

The destiny of the world is determined less by the battles that are lost and won than by the stories it loves and believes in.

— Harold Goddard,
*The Meaning of
Shakespeare, Vol. II*

STANLEY

"I had to fight some procrastination to start this exercise," Stanley admitted.

"Why do you think it was tough for you to start?" I asked him. This is one of the most common questions for me to ask in my initial sessions with clients. Even though most people understand the importance of self-knowledge in achieving their goals, I have found that many people have become so focused on the "crisis du jour" in a hypercompetitive environment that they find it hard to step back and consider their careers from a big-picture perspective. The bad news is that this reluctance to look at the bigger picture usually kicks in precisely when people need this perspective the most. The good news is that clients who report battling fierce internal resistance to getting started with this work are often the ones who come bounding into my office later to tell me about the life-changing realizations they have had when they finally got on with it. Stanley was no exception.

"I've been through a series of bosses," Stanley lamented as he launched into his concerns, "and none of them seems to be terribly fond of me. This began to feel like a full-blown crisis a few weeks ago when I was told I'm now going to report to this new guy who's younger and doesn't understand the business half as well as I do," he continued anxiously. "What's worse, if I don't get promoted, I'm never going to make the kind of money I need to give my wife the option of at least working part-time so she can spend more time with our kids. She's pregnant again, her job is draining her, and even though she never says it directly, I think she's angry that she has to keep working."

"How do you know she's angry about this if she hasn't told you directly?"

"Well... the other night we went to a dinner party and met some new neighbors. The next morning I innocently asked what the woman

> *Being a human being — in the sense of being born to the human species — must be defined in terms of becoming a human being . . . a baby is only potentially a human being, and must grow into humanness in the society and the culture, the family.*
>
> — Abraham Maslow

in this couple did for a living, and my wife replied icily, 'She stays home with her kids. She doesn't have to work.' The edge in my wife's voice terrified me. It's not that my wife isn't willing to help as a financial partner in our marriage — she's always been great that way — it's just that the politics at her firm is so intense right now I know her job is making her nuts. I really wish I could make enough money so she didn't have to subject herself to that while she's trying to be there emotionally for our kids."

One of the most poignant aspects of doing the Personal Tree of Life exercise is that it addresses the vital question of how a client's professional satisfaction is affected by his or her partner's priorities. Since an authentic definition of success encompasses not only the work you are doing but also what you are working *for,* your partner's abilities and dreams must be factored in along with your own.

"What do you and your wife want to do?"

"It's a tough question to tackle because, lately, I think I'm getting depressed. This makes it tough to consider my options creatively. I know I'm good at what I do, and I don't really think I want to leave my job, but getting passed over for promotion has caused me to fantasize about quitting all the time. The truth is that I'm not sure that's a realistic option short-term. I need to support my family. However, I'm worried that my wife and I are both struggling with burnout."

"It sounds like not being able to think clearly about your options is part of the problem," I told him.

"And how!" he sighed. "Realizing this is what helped me fight my way through my procrastination and get this exercise done. I told my wife that I needed a couple of hours over the weekend. I went into my study with a stack of photos and just stared at them for a little while, not quite sure how to begin. Then, I just started laying things out in rows like you suggested, and the exercise started 'doing' me."

"What was the most powerful insight you got from doing this exercise?" I asked him.

Stanley's voice softened as he told me, "The big thing that I hadn't thought about in years was what a hole it had left in my life when my

My mother is the one who made me work, made me believe that one day it would be possible for me to walk without braces.

—Wilma Rudolph

dad died. He passed away when I was ten, and I'm not sure my mom and I ever fully recovered. My two little sisters were only four and two at the time, so they didn't really understand what was going on. I was left as the man of the family, and I never felt like I could cut it."

"How did losing your dad make you question your own ability to succeed?"

Stanley's normally rapid speech slowed down, and he chose his words thoughtfully as he said, "My dad had his own printing company, and everybody loved him. He was a leader in the community, and he took such great care of our family. Looking at pictures of my dad made me want to start crying — I miss him so much. I'm also afraid that I can never be as successful as he was. Whenever I think of him, I realize that I have so much to live up to that I just get paralyzed."

"Does your mother understand the powerful impact that losing your father has had on your professional self-confidence?" I asked him gently.

Stanley pondered this question silently for a few moments. "I'm not sure my mom thinks about what's going on with any of her kids that deeply," he told me. "Struggling with her own inner demons has been a full-time job for her since we lost my dad. When I started working with the pictures of my mom, I realized how stubborn, risk averse, and fiercely intelligent she is.

"As I did this exercise, it sure hit me like a thunderbolt that I'm a lot more like her than I'd care to admit," he confessed. "I mean, after all, she was the only one there to raise me — it makes sense that I'd take on more than a few of her traits. It's painful to realize that I've adopted a lot of the attitudes that I'm always criticizing her for. Realizing this was a bummer. Neither one of us has much of a personal vision. The scariest part of losing my dad is that we all looked to him to lead the way in almost every area. After Dad died, my mom was searching frantically for outside advice about how to raise us and how to react to life's challenges in general. This left her much more worried about what other people thought of her than what she thought of herself. We both worry way too much about what other people think," he told me.

What a strange thing is memory, and hope; one looks backward and the other looks forward. The one is of today, and the other is of tomorrow. Memory is history recorded in [us], memory is a painter, it paints pictures of the past and of the day.

— **Grandma Moses**

"Tell me more about the relationship between your parents when your father was living. From your perspective, did their marriage feel like a romantic union, a business partnership, or both?" I asked him.

"The relationship between my mom and dad had its good and bad points," Stanley told me. "Dad took care of Mom too well, I think. She never worked, she never understood much about finances, and when Dad was killed in a car accident she sold the business quickly because she was afraid she wouldn't be able to run it — and I was certainly too young. Basically, when she lost my dad, she lost her sense of her own priorities in life. Realizing this helped me see that there are some important parallels between how my mom reacted to the stress of losing my dad and how I am reacting to the stress of losing my sense of prestige on the job.

"I had no idea how many of my career choices were driven by what other people thought of me," Stanley admitted. "I've never thought of myself as a particularly insecure person, but as I started answering these questions, I realized that looking good to everyone, from my colleagues to my neighbors, had been totally ruling my life for the past couple of years."

"And you see this as similar to the way your mother reacted to losing your dad?"

"Yes, particularly when I think of the tough conversations I keep having with my wife right now," Stanley confessed. "She hates her job and she wants to spend more time with our kids, but we both worry about keeping up with our peers both as businesspeople and as parents. The more I think about this, I realize that our fears aren't just about money. Between the two of us, we've always managed to get by. It's just that living and working in New York, all we can afford is a small apartment, and we are constantly exposed to images of conspicuous consumption. It starts to seem like you *need* to have all that stuff — especially where your kids are concerned. The peer pressure is endless. The parties, the fancy vacations — I hate the idea of not being able to give my kids all the 'advantages' that other parents seem to be able to offer their children."

"So, are you telling me that your concern about what other people think of you is beginning to have an impact on the values you are passing on to your kids?"

"Absolutely," Stanley told me, looking troubled. "I've noticed that there are some side effects to giving in to our kids' demands all the time that are beginning to trouble my wife and me. It's not just that my wife seems cranky about going to a job she's gotten tired of, it's that this crankiness is rubbing off on my kids and their outlook on life. They are rarely grateful for what they do get these days, and they get so cross if we don't 'snap to it' and pay for whatever they seem to want immediately that it's making us wonder."

"What can you do to help your kids develop a less materialistic value system?"

"Part of me wants to take the whole family off for a camping vacation in the woods or something just to get back to nature," Stanley told me as he gazed at the trees outside my office window. "This would be a real contrast from the lavish vacations we usually take to an expensive theme park. While the kids would protest initially, spending some time in nature would give us a chance to focus on something besides how we are being entertained."

"Like each other?" I asked.

"Yeah," he said smiling, "like each other. For that matter, I want to spend more time with my wife. I'm beginning to realize that she can probably start working part-time in a few months, as long as we are willing to make a few lifestyle changes. One of the biggest problems I'm struggling with is not lack of money — it's about developing the self-confidence I need to stop worrying all the time about what other people think of me and start living by the values that I think are important. One of these values is spending more time with my family. Another is not letting the pressure of what my colleagues think of me keep me preoccupied and anxious when I am at home. My mom was always so worried that even when she was with us, she wasn't really there, if you know what I mean."

"How is that feeling of pressure affecting the way you react on the job now?" I asked.

The most important thing that parents can teach their children is how to get along without them.

— Frank A. Clark

Our virtues and vices couple with one another, and beget children that resemble both their parents.

— George Savile,
Marquess of Halifax

"It's making me paranoid and jumpy," he admitted. "Before doing this exercise, I was convinced that the toxic office politics that started after my firm merged with a former competitor was the main reason I had been repeatedly passed over for promotion. I'm not saying this isn't a factor, but I think some self-esteem issues have been holding me back as well."

"And what do you think these are?" I asked.

"I think my constant worrying keeps other people from seeing me as a leader," he told me. "After all, leaders live by their own vision and values — even if that doesn't please everyone else all the time. When I think of how I judge other people, I realize that I look at how they react under pressure and whether they are able to be true to themselves personally as well as professionally. If I could be a bit less anxious all the time, my boss would be more likely to believe that I could manage other people under stress.

"After I was done with this exercise, I told my wife I was going out to pick up some groceries for dinner. She could tell I just needed some time alone, and she gave me such a loving kiss before I left that I almost lost it. I drove to a park near our home, parked the car, and just sat there for about a half-hour. I realized that my problems are a lot bigger than my job. I'd always thought that if I just got the next promotion, that it was all going to be okay. Now I realize that, if I don't stop trying to be my dad and start trying to be myself, I'm never going to be happy. The trouble is that I've been trying to be him for so long, I'm not sure how to do anything else. However, becoming more aware of the way my background has influenced the way I think about my career is a big step forward for me."

The critical responsibility for the generation you're in is to help provide the shoulders, the direction, and the support for those generations who come behind.

— Gloria Dean Randle Scott

Like Stanley, many people have strong emotional reactions to this exercise. Please be gentle with yourself. This exercise is meant to alleviate self-blame, not foster it. We were all conditioned by the systems we were born into. As children we had about as much control over this process as we did over when the sun came up. However, conditioning thrives in the shadows, and when we become aware of the patterns in our lives, conditioning has less ability to influence us in ways that we no longer desire.

I realized the importance of understanding the way our families influence our perspective about professional success when I was completing my externship at the Ackerman Institute for Couples and Family Therapy. Early in my coaching career, I had decided to get additional clinical training in family therapy because the turf wars that I was encountering on Wall Street were as emotionally colorful as a day in divorce court. One of the toughest formal parts of counseling training is that, at some point in the process, you are subjected to the same kind of analysis that you put your clients through. It's the emotional equivalent of having to eat your own cooking, and it fosters some much-needed empathy about what the client experiences when they seek help.

One afternoon, it was my turn to be the subject while the group of therapists I was in training with analyzed my family background. As an experienced public speaker, I smugly assumed that this process was going to be a snap. I was as shocked as anyone when I felt my face flush and I found I was fighting to keep the emotion out of my voice as I explained how my lonely climb through the political hierarchy of Wall Street paralleled my lonely experience as an only child. I was horrified when I heard my voice crack as I described what it was like frequently to be the target of other people's jealousy. I looked up furtively to make sure that the slip of my mask of professionalism had not been noticed by my peers. But they had noticed, and I saw that several of the therapists in my training group were crying for me — something I could not do for myself at that point.

The love and acceptance I felt from that group of therapists during our training years taught me some lessons that were radically

After a certain age, the more one becomes oneself, the more obvious one's family traits become.

— **Marcel Proust**

The pain of leaving those you grow to love is only the prelude to understanding yourself and others.

— **Shirley MacLaine**

Don't limit your child to your learning, for he was born in another time.

— Anonymous

How strange when an illusion dies, it's as though you've lost a child.

— Judy Garland

different from those I had learned at corporate leadership retreats. In leadership seminars, top performers learn, "never let them see you sweat." While it's vital to be a consummate performer to succeed in today's workforce, to get ahead without losing yourself in the process you must be able to stop performing when the presentation is over. You must be real — especially with yourself. We all sweat.

To achieve your career goals, you must be clear about what they are and why they are meaningful to you. Even if doing the Personal Tree of Life exercise helps you discover that you're not sure what direction you want to go with your career, by clarifying the way others may have influenced you, you have come that much closer to identifying your authentic desires.

Money is one of the most emotional topics in our culture today. Credit card companies, brokerage firms, and professional financial planners devote millions of dollars to providing clients with spreadsheets tracking everything from the asset allocation of their investments to the history of their spending habits to help them make "logical" investment decisions. The irony is that there is little that is logical about many people's relationship with money. Money taps into our fantasies about pleasure and power — and into our most primal drives for safety and security.

Vagueness about monetary expectations contributes to professional inertia. Many of us have done goal-setting exercises and have a pretty good idea about what we would do with our lives if money were not a consideration. However, those of us who are not independently wealthy must consider the need to support ourselves and our families while charting our career strategy. Without having a practical plan in place for how you are going to get paid for doing the job you love — or how you are going to fund your own business — you will miss a vital component of turning your dreams into your reality.

Throughout my career, I have learned to listen very carefully to my clients' hopes and fears about money. As a portfolio manager, I knew that since there were so many talented money managers competing for business, the best of us had to connect with potential clients at an emotional level. When someone hires a portfolio manager they are not just paying for logic, they are paying for peace of mind.

As a coach, it's even more vital that I understand the way the emotional dynamics surrounding money influence my clients' decisions. Coaching clients wrestle with questions such as, "Will this job provide me with a secure financial future? Will I make enough money to travel

CHAPTER 2

Your Monetary Detective Work

if I freelance? Should I invest my personal savings in the stock of the company I work for?" Although these all sound like logical questions, they also tap into the fantasies and fears of those asking them.

People limit their professional potential when they don't do the monetary detective work necessary to be honest about how much money they need to feel secure enough to pursue their authentic career goals. For example, some clients whom I have worked with have managed to get independent films financed and books published (accomplishments that were life dreams for them) by keeping their living expenses low and supporting themselves through consulting or part-time work that left them free to pursue their creative ambitions. Sadly, I've seen other people remain trapped in dead-end careers for years because they believed they could not afford to leave their jobs. These clients frequently discover, once they take an objective look at their living expenses, that emotional factors have been holding them back more than economic ones.

Some things in life are expensive financially, and others are expensive emotionally. Almost anything is too costly if it comes between you and your ability to realize your full potential. Truly understanding your relationship with money dramatically reduces the risk that you will look back on your career when it is too late to change course and be forced to muse, "I wonder if I could have..."

The second exercise in the Awareness Stage comes from a seminar that I originally designed to teach financial planners a more in-depth method of understanding their clients' concerns and goals. The feedback from this exercise was so positive that, over the years, I redesigned it for more general use.

The old Indians say that if you give away something that's important to you, your life is renewed. It means that you have the things; the things don't have you. If you can't give away your possessions, they will destroy you.

— Carl A. Hammerschlag

EXERCISE:

YOUR NET WORTH COMFORT ZONE

It is vital that you be clear with yourself about the emphasis you place on personal wealth in setting your professional goals. If you don't do this, you may find yourself wasting years waffling between various idealistic career scenarios, only to abandon your dreams at the first whiff of financial fear. Understanding what I call your Net Worth Comfort Zone will clarify your risk tolerance when dealing with a temporary pay cut or an uncertain income stream in order to create a meaningful career.

One of the most widely used terms that was popularized in the internet boom to describe the amount of cash flow it takes to keep a business functioning on a monthly basis was the organization's "burn rate." While this term may seem tired for many of us because we've heard it so often (not to mention the fact that we feel tired when we start thinking of financial resources draining away!), it is particularly helpful in understanding the way financial pressures may be influencing your career decisions. In this chapter, you are going to calculate what I call your "personal burn rate." This is the amount of money it takes for you to maintain your lifestyle on a monthly basis. It should include your rent or mortgage payments, your utility bills, your insurance, what you spend on food and transportation, and a reasonable approximation of what you spend on impulse purchases, entertainment, and vacations.

It takes many people a few days to remember all the things they spend money on in the course of a month (whoops! I forgot the health club bill...whoops! I forgot the dry cleaning bill), so I suggest that you give yourself a few days to review your checking account and credit card bills and revise your list of relevant expenses accordingly.

Once you have a list of your relevant expenses, calculate the amount of money your current lifestyle requires every month and compare this amount with your current income stream. If you haven't done this exercise before, the results can be quite surprising. As one client told me, "I was shocked to find that my family's lifestyle cost more monthly than it did to run my small company when it was a start-up."

After you have calculated a reasonable approximation of your personal burn rate, answer the following three sets of questions:

Life begets life, energy creates energy. It is by spending oneself that one becomes rich.

— Sarah Bernhardt

A wise man will make more opportunities than he finds.

— Sir Francis Bacon

YOUR PERSONAL BURN RATE

1. How much money do I need to support myself (and my family) monthly and annually?
2. Does my current job or career plan provide sufficient cash flow to meet my immediate financial needs?
3. Do other sources of income (such as inheritance, savings, investments) meet my cash-flow needs if my current career plan does not provide sufficient funds?

YOUR FINANCIAL FEELINGS

1. How predictable do I need my cash flow to be in order to feel emotionally comfortable? Do I need a regular salary to feel satisfied, or am I comfortable with earning very little in the short term for the promise of a large investment payoff in the future?
2. Does my family need my cash flow to be more predictable than I do to feel safe?
3. Are my ideas about the amount of money I need to earn to feel financially secure realistic, or are they emotionally influenced by the accomplishments of family members or peers with whom I compare myself?
4. Are my views about wealth and financial security enhancing my enjoyment of my life and my career, or are they limiting me?
5. How much of my personal satisfaction is tied to the amount of money I earn? Why is this the case?

A great deal of current "positive thinking" is premised on selecting only that aspect of your story that relates to your apparent prosperity and getting what "you" want out of life. The problem with this is: which of the [many] "yous" is doing the wanting?

— Jean Houston

YOUR FINANCIAL FUTURE

1. What role does money play in my long-term life goals?
2. How much money do I think I will need to save to retire comfortably?
3. How does my career strategy coincide with my long-term financial goals?

Catherine's experience doing the Net Worth Comfort Zone exercise illustrates how this exercise can help clarify the role that money plays when people are considering their career options. Catherine works in public relations. She came for coaching because, in spite of making professional progress, her relationship with money was limiting her career options. She was concerned that her spending habits were keeping her from taking the steps necessary to start her own firm and were putting her long-term financial security at risk.

We are shaped and fashioned by what we love.

— Goethe

CATHERINE

"I'm often walking around under a cloud of guilt," Catherine told me. "My father is always reminding me that I am making more at the beginning of my career than he was earning at the end of his. I know he's worried about my having enough to live on when I retire. Even though I realize he's got my best interests at heart, he makes me so anxious when this topic comes up that sometimes I wish he would keep his opinions to himself. Of course, then I feel guilty about reacting this way because how can I expect him to understand the emotional pressures of being a single working woman — much less the therapeutic value of going to a good shoe sale?"

"What are the biggest pressures you are facing?" I asked her.

"Well, frankly, it costs me more to live in a one-bedroom in the city and maintain my current lifestyle than it seems to cost some of the friends I grew up with to raise their families. This worries me. What's worse, even though my salary has just managed to cover my expenses over the past few years, shopping has become the way I ease my stress when the politics at my office gets intense. What's most alarming is that I've noticed that shopping to deal with stress is affecting more than my bank balance — it's also affecting my career choices."

"In what way?"

Life itself is the proper binge.

— Julia Child

For where your treasure is,
there will your heart
be also.

— Matthew 6:21

"I realized a few years ago that I knew enough about my business and had strong enough client contacts in the industry to start my own firm. However, when I think about the initial drop in my earning power, I get terrified. I shop on the Internet to ease my stress when clients don't return my calls. This may sound silly, but I'm concerned that the stress of starting my own business might be too much for me if I didn't have the extra cash to take the edge off by shopping."

No problem is silly if it's holding you back from pursuing your dreams. I've met many people who have learned that by becoming more aware of their spending habits, they have been able to save enough money to start a company, become a freelancer, pursue a second degree, and generally finance a life that will support their ambitions. Simply by becoming more conscious of their spending habits and clarifying their goals, many people have been able to rebuild their lives much more economically than they had believed possible. "Are you telling me that if your spending habits were more under control, you would want to leave your current job and go out on your own?" I asked her.

"I really don't believe in what I'm doing anymore, and I don't take much pride in my work," she said, her voice trembling slightly. "I do take pride in having a job, but I know I'm missing out on building a meaningful career. I had initially moved to this city because I was sure that I would quickly make my fortune, marry the man of my dreams, and be on my way to the good life — whatever *that* is. However, this rather vague life plan seems to be taking much longer than I had expected. Even when I began this job, I realized that I was going to be taking a financial gamble to pay the rent on my expensive one-bedroom apartment here. The vicious cycle is that I've gotten increasingly slick at justifying random purchases to take the edge off when I start to feel trapped."

I'm amazed at how much
of what we call interior
decorating is just
subconscious altar building.

— Luisha Teish

Whether you're male or female, it's important to bear in mind that the rapid changes in our economy may make you the primary bread-winner during segments of your working life. Being mindful of your finances so that you can invest in your retirement portfolio (or simply save more money) is important, but clarifying your relationship with money so that you can invest in your career is one of the most important decisions you will make in your life.

"We all need to have some fun," I reassured her. "Did calculating your personal burn rate help you separate the purchases that bring you pleasure from the ones that leave you with a guilt hangover?"

Catherine paused for a moment and then responded thoughtfully, "Doing this exercise helped me realize that something just wasn't adding up. I'm not a greedy person, and I'm not a snob. I come from a Jewish family with a strong work ethic and good family values. However, when I considered the link between my spending problems and my family history, I remembered that my mom and dad had had such huge fights over money when I was a teenager that I was afraid they were going to get a divorce. The problems between my parents stemmed from the fact that my father's business wasn't as profitable as he had hoped it would be, and my mother was resentful that she couldn't throw the kind of lavish bat mitzvah party for me that she had always dreamed of. While she never said it, I was convinced my mother felt that our family would have been more financially secure if my father hadn't tried to start his own business. Suddenly, the pieces of the puzzle began to fall into place. I've always been an extremely competent executive, but the perfectionism that has gotten me ahead in a tough industry is based on some deep personal insecurities. Part of me has always believed that if I'm not accepted in the corporate hierarchy, I won't be able to make it."

"So are you telling me that you think that because your dad wasn't able to make it as an entrepreneur, that you won't be able to either?" I asked her.

"That's a belief that's been driving me, for sure," she said, nodding vigorously. "And that's one reason my spending habits get out of control. It's as if I tell myself, 'What's the point of saving to build your own business? You could never do it anyway.'"

"Do you really believe that?" I challenged her.

Life is a process of becoming, a combination of states that we have to go through. Where people fail is that they wish to elect a state and remain in it. This is a kind of death.

— Anaïs Nin

"If I did," she said, looking me right in the eye, "I wouldn't be here. There's very little security in my industry right now. People are losing their jobs so regularly that we all have to be entrepreneurial in this market — even if we work for someone else. In a crazy way, there are days when it feels like it would be safer to work for myself. At least then I'd know what senior management was planning to try and stay competitive — I'd *be* senior management. Not knowing what our bosses are thinking or when we could lose our jobs leaves everyone in my group feeling pretty insecure, and of course, that makes office politics fierce."

"But is your spending easing the pressure for you, or adding to it?"

"It does a bit of both, if I'm honest about it," she told me. "One of the main ways I compensate for feeling so vulnerable on the inside when the corporate politics heat up is that I keep things impeccable on the outside. My wardrobe takes a huge chunk out of my salary, but I feel I need it to compensate for the inner poverty I feel. But I'm afraid it's also keeping me from focusing on what I want most out of life."

"And what would that be for you?" I asked her.

"I feel awkward admitting this, but I think I'm overcompensating for the stress I feel because I haven't been able to find the right guy and build a family of my own. I have a state-of-the-art designer kitchen with no food in the refrigerator. It's a metaphor for my life," she said softly.

"Why do you feel awkward admitting this?" I asked her.

"I'm afraid to tell people this, because I'm afraid that if they know I want a family, they will think that my career is not a priority."

"Don't you have room in your life for more than one priority?" I asked her gently.

Suddenly, Catherine's somber expression vanished and she broke into a wide grin as she asked, "Are you suggesting that as a talented woman I might be able to balance work and a family?"

"Absolutely."

"Next you're going to tell me I can walk and chew gum at the same time!" she said laughing.

We are living beyond our means. As a people we have developed a life-style that is draining the earth of its priceless and irreplaceable resources without regard for the future of our children and people all around the world.

— Margaret Mead

"Well, as we all know, it's a bit more complicated than that," I continued, impressed by her emotional resilience and wit when confronting a tough topic. "Men want balance as much as women do these days. Protecting our resources of time and energy has become critical for every person who wants to genuinely enjoy life in an era when there are so many demands on our time and attention. To make the most of your resources long-term, it sounds like you may need to pay special attention to the relationship between spending and stress."

Catherine was silent for a few minutes before she said thoughtfully, "As I considered the way that my financial fears were affecting my long-term goals, I realized that I haven't been able to give myself the time to have a decent social life because I'm always anxious about the next deadline at work. I think this anxiety also feeds insecurity that keeps me from starting my own business. In many ways, I wear the prestige of working for a big-name firm the way that I wear a designer dress. All these related concerns stem from the central belief that, if my dad couldn't do it, how can I believe that I can succeed by going into business on my own?"

"So what can you do with this insight?"

"I can start investing in what I need to feel good on the inside for a while. This will help me find better ways to take the edge off than blowing money on clothes I don't even have the time to wear. What helped me most in this exercise was putting my financial numbers down on paper and doing the math. I'm going to start working on a rational plan to start my own business and create the wealth and flexibility I will need to someday enjoy a family of my own. Making my life dream less vague is a powerful step for me."

Understanding the way your relationship with money influences your professional choices is vital to achieving authentic success.

Sometimes people can hunger for more than bread. It is possible that our children, our husband, our wife do not hunger for bread, do not need clothes, do not lack a house. But are we equally sure that none of them feels alone, abandoned, neglected, needing some affection? That, too, is poverty.

— **Mother Teresa**

Men who borrow their opinions can never repay their debts.

— George Savile, Marquess of Halifax

To put a realistic career strategy in place, you must be able to accept your tolerance for taking risks and for financial uncertainty. Many executives deny themselves permission to pursue career opportunities that ultimately would be extremely rewarding because they fear dealing with the financial uncertainty that the first couple of years would entail. Other clients struggle with tremendous stress because they believe that their partners and families need them to produce enough income to support a certain lifestyle. Often, the financial desires of such families are related to a longing for security in an insecure world far more than they relate to any type of materialism.

Like many of the exercises in this book, the Net Worth Comfort Zone exercise is derived from my personal as well as from my professional experience. One evening during my years as a portfolio manager in Boston, I was walking home and musing about the number of friends in other industries who would shyly ask me for investment advice. A close friend of mine, Nancy, had pulled out her brokerage report while we were having pizza the night before and had asked me what I thought. As we discussed her portfolio, I found myself discussing her emotional expectations of her portfolio as well as the merits of various asset classes. While I was happy to give Nancy my perspective, doing this with a friend made me realize that I had neglected my own feelings about my financial situation for some time.

Life is an arrow — therefore you must know what mark to aim at and how to use the bow.

— Henry Van Dyke

The more I thought about this, the more I realized that even though my career was devoted to helping other people have the financial resources necessary to achieve their life goals, I'd been incredibly vague in dealing with my own emotional relationship with money. For years, even though I banked a certain percentage of my Wall Street salary, I wasn't focused on the specific amount of money it would take for me to provide for my own long-term financial needs and to get the experience I needed to pursue a second career. This was particularly awkward for me to come to terms with because, as a portfolio manager, I spent my days helping other people grapple with issues that I hadn't resolved in my own life. If I hadn't eventually forced myself to come to terms with exactly how much I earned, and exactly how much it would cost me to support myself, I'd never have had the freedom to consider making a career transition from my portfolio management career in Boston to my job as a director of consultant relations in New York. The hard financial facts I faced making a transition from the "buy side" to the "sell side" on Wall Street were tough to face (as a female portfolio manager in the early 1990s, even though I earned a good salary, I was paid significantly less than my male counterparts), but worth the effort. This financial self-scrutiny formed the foundation I eventually built on to figure out how much money I would need to survive while I pursued a second master's degree to become an executive coach.

Reflecting on your Net Worth Comfort Zone is designed to give you some valuable insight into what money means to you and to those you love. Such insight is vital for anyone who hopes to maximize his or her professional success. Great careers are built by finding a job that gives you a chance to express your unique talents and abilities. If your life choices are dictated solely by the size of your paycheck, the price you pay is your unexplored dreams.

If we are to achieve a richer culture, rich in contrasting values, we must recognize the whole gamut of human potentialities, and so weave a less arbitrary social fabric, one in which each diverse human gift will find a fitting place.

— **Margaret Mead**

CHAPTER 3

The Mental Alchemy of Releasing the "Shoulds"

Up to this point, the Awareness Stage has been about doing the mental detective work necessary to understand how your background has been shaping your career choices. This self-exploration is a prerequisite for clarifying the distinction between what others may have led you to believe that you "should" do with your career and what you actually desire.

Making this distinction isn't just a matter of logic; it can be a highly emotional process for many people. I am always wary of organizational behavior specialists who shy away from the role that an individual's emotional reactions play in his or her professional performance. The one thing that all of us have in common is our feelings. They are the glue that holds our world together.

Our most deeply held values and beliefs are nothing more than our most emotionally saturated thoughts. Thus, when we get down to the serious business of working through limiting beliefs that may be retarding our professional growth, we will need to deal with some powerful feelings that have been fueling these beliefs for some time. Changing the belief system behind our perspective of reality can be as painful emotionally as severing a limb is physically. One of the ways we avoid the pain of examining our most familiar beliefs is by convincing ourselves that we "should" operate according to this belief system.

Whenever we say to ourselves, "I should..." we are speaking out of an internalized belief system that reflects our inability to trust ourselves. The bummer about "shoulds" is that when we are dominated by them, we are also dominated by the fear of being rejected or abandoned in some way, because that's the core emotional fear that activates many of them. These ongoing fears leave many of us drained and exhausted.

Part of the work in this stage is to take a deeper look not only at what the thoughts swirling just below the surface of our consciousness are but also at what they are doing to us daily. Those pesky little shoulds — "I should lose weight…I should stop smoking…I should have a bigger house…I should spend more time with my kids…I should be making as much money as my sister" — that keep nipping away at our psyches are the psychic equivalent of Chinese water torture. Every time we use the word *should,* either mentally or verbally, not only are we giving our power away, we are also losing energy that is vital to our ability to take creative ownership of our careers and our lives.

The trick to releasing the shoulds is realizing that they have an emotional component as well as an intellectual one. You can make a list of the shoulds that you need to release, but you will be making this list over and over unless you deal with the feelings that keep them clinging to your psyche like Velcro. Obviously, listing them is just going to remind you of ways you are falling short of the glorious role you are playing to prove you are "good enough." You need to try something more strategic.

I got the name for this exercise from a client who told me that when she became discouraged, she often realized that she was having a "should attack." To help retrain her thought process, she actually got down on her knees and pulled the weeds out of her flowerbed. She visualized herself pulling the "shoulds" out of her psyche as she pulled the weeds out of the ground. This client developed a physical ritual that got to the heart of the work for her. Likewise, we need to physically release the emotions connected to our shoulds if we are going to make meaningful progress in thinning these "mental weeds."

The final two exercises in the Awareness Stage are designed to help you begin to release your litany of shoulds and identify your authentic priorities. Many people feel a tremendous surge of energy while doing this work. When you release your shoulds you finally stop giving yourself those messages that drain you of the energy you need to move forward.

I often marvel how it is that though each man loves himself beyond all else, he should yet value his own opinion of himself less than others.

— Marcus Aurelius

EXERCISE:

WEEDING THE "SHOULDS"

Find a picture of yourself as a small child. Next, take your journal, notebook, or laptop and find a place where you can be around children.

"Kids!?" I've had incredulous clients thunder (these are usually the ones who are not parents; parents get this exercise before I'm through describing it). "I'm a busy person," I had one client respond in a huff. "I don't have time for this! I have important career decisions to make and I'm on a *deadline!*"

The reason it's important to do this exercise around kids is that they reawaken an energy that has been dormant in many of us for far too long — the energy of gentleness. Spending time with children reminds you that a vital part of getting in touch with your authentic self is learning to be gentle with yourself. Phrases such as "*Get* that client meeting or you can *get* a new job! Are you an idiot? Didn't you hear me *tell* you?" are the types of harsh messages that too many of us have become accustomed to in our jobs. What's worse, since the way we speak to others is a direct reflection of the way we speak to ourselves, the mean-spirited behavior and verbal abuse that takes place in many workplaces reflects a growing problem — we are suffering from a gentleness deficiency.

The limiting beliefs and self-doubts that plague most of us are formidable opponents. One of the most effective ways of dealing with these harsh internal messages is to learn to question every single should and limiting belief with the gentle innocence of children. It was only when we were children that our psyches were malleable enough to absorb these beliefs without questioning them. By acknowledging our limiting beliefs and honoring the way they may have served us in the past, we align mentally with what's going on inside us. Telling ourselves that we are "wrong" to hold the beliefs we do or denying them altogether just keeps us fighting a losing battle. Now that I've explained why you need to be around children to do this exercise (spending some time in a public park is a great way to do this), let me

*Man is born free,
and everywhere
he is in chains.*

— Jean Jacques Rousseau

*Most people are other
people. Their thoughts are
someone else's opinions,
their lives a mimicry,
their passions a quotation.*

— Oscar Wilde

be a bit more specific about how this exercise works. While you need to be around a bunch of kids, you're also going to need some privacy for part of this exercise to do a bit of written reflection. This means that whether you are spending time with a friend's kids or your own, you are going to need a buddy who helps you take a "time-out" in the corner of your room while you write in your journal.

The first part of this exercise is easy — just get a feel for the kids. If you are in a public park, notice how they run and play and interact with each other. If you are with some kids you know, get right down there on the floor and play with them. Notice how they react when they want something, how they recover after a fall, and how much they trust their caregivers to take care of them. When you are ready, take a time-out and take out the picture of yourself as a child. It's time to reflect on what you imagine you were like when you were about the age of the children around you. Now, from the perspective of that child you were in the past, take out your journal or laptop and start listing your shoulds. Just write them all down as fast as you can. For example:

I *should* make more money.
I *should* have a better car.
I *should* get married.
I *should* lose weight so my favorite jeans fit.

List as many as you can as fast as you can; don't bother making sense of them yet. Please be sure to include your thoughts about the professional role you "should" play in life:

I *should* stay at my current firm.
I *should* start my own business.
I *should* learn a second language.
I *should* be teaching more classes.

Once you start winding down, take a look at this list from the perspective you would have had as a child. As vividly as possible, try to imagine yourself as a small child sitting next to you reviewing each item on this list and asking with the innocence that only kids possess

> *The world is full of people who have stopped listening to themselves or have listened only to their neighbors to learn what they ought to do, how they ought to behave, and what the values are that they should be living for.*
>
> — Joseph Campbell

why you should do all these things. If you can't explain why a particular goal is on your list, you might consider weeding it out. Bear in mind that a child is likely to ask why doing a particular thing will be fun for you and how it will make you happy. If any of your shoulds can't pass that test, it's time to weed them out!

Take your time with Weeding the "Shoulds." Some people can do this exercise in an afternoon. However, other clients have reported that they kept coming up with new and subtler shoulds over the course of a week. Getting through this exercise successfully is critical to building the self-acceptance necessary to proceed to the next stage, Emotional Ownership.

This exercise helped Susan, an aspiring fashion designer, get in touch with feelings she might otherwise have suppressed.

SUSAN

"At first, when I did this exercise, everything I came up with was related to the problems I'm having with office politics," Susan told me. "I realized that I have a punishing inner voice that kept repeating things like, 'I should be more self-confident.' 'I should stand up to other people,' 'I should be more direct.'"

"What are the political problems that trigger this inner criticism?" I asked her.

Susan sighed and told me, "There's a painful irony to being a designer these days. Even though my industry relies on the creativity of its staff to make money, the work environment doesn't always nurture creative people. To get people to pay attention to my designs, I constantly have to make presentations to people in our firm who have more business experience than I do — but less imagination. That's tough on its own, but add to this the pressure of competing with other designers to get my ideas into production, and sometimes I get stressed to the max. You see, I'm a sensitive person to begin with. But as an artist, I feel like I give birth to my designs. I really put my heart and soul into what I create. When somebody attacks my ideas, I almost feel like they are attacking my children. I beat myself up so much over the way I blow internal presentations that I often wonder if I'm in the right profession, even though I love my work."

"How are you blowing these presentations?" I asked her.

"I always seem to give my power away to other people," she said sadly. If somebody in authority disagrees with me, I seem to lose my voice, my mind goes blank, and I start feeling like a loser. Actually, I think what's really going on is that I'm mad. However, whenever I'm angry, I simply shut down. Then the litany of 'shoulds' kicks in and I find that I'm beating myself up more effectively than anyone else possibly could."

"Did doing this exercise surrounded by kids give you any perspective?" I asked her.

"Absolutely. It was amazing to see how spontaneous the kids were with their feelings," she told me. "One minute they were furious with each other, and the next all was forgiven. As I watched them, I realized that one thing I needed to come to terms with was how much of my spontaneity and personal power I had suppressed in an effort to keep my anger from showing."

"What were the shoulds you listed that may prevent you from expressing your anger?"

Susan gripped her notes tightly as she read, "'I should endure hardships with grace,' 'I should do God's will,' 'I should be grateful for all I have.'"

"Where do you think you got those messages?" I asked her.

"This is all family stuff," she told me. "My father was a small-town parish priest, and my mother made many sacrifices to raise three daughters on a preacher's salary. There was a lot of pressure to perform, because Dad's livelihood depended on us being 'good little children of

Perhaps loving something is the only starting place there is for making your life your own.

— Alice Koller

Always be a first-rate version of yourself, instead of a second-rate version of somebody else.

— Judy Garland

God.' Of course, it was my parents defining what was 'good,' but since my dad was a representative of the Lord, who were we to question his authority?"

"Did anyone in your family ever get a little angry about all that sacrificing?"

"We all did. However, from our earliest years we were also indoctrinated with the idea that we should be humble, obedient, and serve God in all things. We had wealthy members of the congregation over for dinner regularly, and we all knew it was important to be very, very good. In our house, being good meant never being angry. After all, we were all part of the show."

"Is this belief that anger is bad connected to the way you give your power away at work?"

"I've been thinking a lot about that," Susan told me. "Not being able to be angry is certainly a key reason that I can't confront people when I need to. It bothers me that I haven't been able to support my ideas with the same passion that goes into my work when I create them."

"When you lose your healthy anger, you lose your voice," I told her gently. "Anger is an important emotion. It's important to be able to confront people in a competitive environment to protect yourself and your ideas."

"Reading over my list of shoulds helped me see that my family training to be obedient and cooperative was part of the reason I have always hated confrontation so much," Susan admitted. "What's more, what my dad wanted and what I thought was 'God's will' got pretty confusing when I was growing up. Listing my shoulds showed me that part of me still believes that I should never express my anger if I want to stay on God's good side. Not only does that keep me from speaking up for myself, it feeds this exhausting amount of guilt. This whole confusing debate in my mind makes me angry at myself — and even angry at God."

"So how has writing these shoulds down helped you the most?" I asked her.

"It's helped me see how illogical some of the beliefs dictating my actions are. I'm amazed when I think of how long some of these limiting ideas have been churning around in the back of my mind — and how long they have been making me anxious. One thing's for sure: I'm going to consciously work on speaking up for what I believe in so I can protect myself and my ideas."

Let's face it — we all want it all! Wealth, power, flexibility... with as little effort on our part as possible, please. Ask most people what their ideal lifestyle would be, and frequently you will hear something along the lines of, "I'd like to earn enough money to set my own work schedule... to have a beautiful home... to spend time with my children... to travel whenever I want...." The list goes on.

This above all:
to thine own self be true.
And it must follow as the
night the day, thou canst not
then be false to any man.

—William Shakespeare

One of the issues that many of us have to confront as we integrate our diverse desires is how to prioritize. When we have a clear picture of what our authentic goals are, as opposed to what we believe we "should" pursue in life, we are able to make temporary sacrifices in the interest of our long-term success without having our energy drained by self-doubt. This is particularly vital in a culture in which we are presented with so many choices and where the media encourages us to "have it all."

One of the first steps in achieving your goals is deciding how much you really want them. When our desire for something is a reflection of our authentic sense of self, we can focus on achieving this goal in a way that maximizes our ability to achieve it. One of the main impediments to success is that many of us have been taught to suppress our passion in favor of the logical arguments we hear from others about what we "should" do. Because of this, many of us become confused trying to separate what we really want from what we have been taught we should want.

Now that you have some experience listing your shoulds, you are ready for the next exercise, which is designed to help you identify the genuine desires that you may have suppressed while making choices based on the values you have internalized from others.

This exercise consists of three parts: reviewing your shoulds, describing your authentic self, and ranking your priorities.

1. Reviewing your shoulds. Basically, your shoulds are a (sometimes harsh) list of beliefs about how you aren't measuring up. The good news here is that all these negative beliefs can be transformed into positive goals that reflect your authentic self. For example, if one of your shoulds takes the form of "I *should* trust my own judgment" this can be transformed into the realization that if you were operating from your authentic self, you would be confident about your decisions and not driven by the need to constantly solicit others' opinions. When you are being your authentic self, you are guided by your genuine values and highest ideals. Go through your list of shoulds, and pick out those that you can transform into characteristics that you feel describe you when you are at your best.

2. Describing your authentic self. After reworking your shoulds into a list of characteristics that define your authentic self, write a description of this self in the third person. Your job here is to write as if your authentic self were a good friend whom you know intimately. Write as much detail as you can about how your authentic self relates to others. What kind of life does he or she have? What are the priorities of your ideal self? As you describe the inner world and the life choices of your authentic self, remember that this description, however genuine, is related in many ways to

It's never too late to be what you might have been.

— George Eliot

Just trust yourself, then you will know how to live.

— Goethe

your concept of your ideal self. Bear in mind that your ideals and desires will constantly change as the world changes.

3. Ranking your priorities. After describing your authentic self, answer the following questions:

- What are the three most important things in your life right now?

- Do you have mixed feelings about any of these priorities?

- Does the way you are living reflect these priorities? If not, why not?

John works in a consulting firm. He found that this exercise helped him to clarify his priorities at a time when his firm was in the process of massive downsizing.

The first rule in opera is the first rule in life; see to everything yourself.

— Dame Nellie Melba

JOHN

"My first stab at reworking the shoulds brought up a lot of financial concerns," John told me. "I had gone on for quite a while writing things like, 'I should make more money,' 'I should review my personal investments,' and 'I should find a job with more security.'

"I know there are many other important issues related to building a meaningful life that I need to deal with besides money. To survive financially, I have to figure out what I want to do, who can pay me to do it, and how I can build on my personal history so the job takes me to the next level in my career. However, everyone I know is so financially panicked right now. I almost can't go to some of the networking groups in my business because the people there are so negative about our industry."

"Remember," I told him, "no matter how negative the people around you may get, it only takes one great opportunity to get to the next level in your career. Separating what you really want from what you have been taught you should want by others will give you a level

Self-love, my liege, is not so vile a sin as self-neglecting.

—William Shakespeare

of focus and authenticity that will help you identify that opportunity and get that job."

"That rings true for me," he said thoughtfully. "The people I meet who are so panicked about money that they are willing to take a job — any job — aren't giving off vibes that are going to be attractive to potential employers."

"Did other areas besides financial fears come up for you when you did this work?" I asked him.

"Well . . . I also noticed that there was a whole subset of shoulds devoted to staying employed by a prestigious organization," he told me.

"Is this related to your concerns about financial security, or are other factors contributing to this belief?" I asked him.

"Security is certainly an issue," he told me, "but the biggest factor is that my family has always been quite impressed that I work for a big-name firm."

"So pleasing your family is a big motivator for you?"

"Oh, without a doubt," John told me. "For example, another area of shoulds that stood out was my belief that I 'should make enough money to help my family.' Growing up, I lived in the shadow of an older brother who could do no wrong in the eyes of my parents. He was the star athlete, and I was the academic nerd. However, a few years ago my brother's fledgling restaurant fell on hard times. The whole family became quite impressed that I was able to lend him enough money to put a down payment on a new home. This was a turning point in the way my family treated me. It was like they began to appreciate me and really see me for the first time."

"Was being appreciated a factor when you considered your life priorities from the perspective of your authentic self?"

"Definitely. What I realized was that my best self was someone who was smart and experienced enough to hold his own in any corporate environment," he told me. "I began realizing that my authentic self would have the self-confidence to find a work atmosphere where I was treated with dignity and respect.

The mass of men lead lives of quiet desperation.

— Henry David Thoreau

There is only one success — to be able to spend your life in your own way.

— Christopher Morley

"The mood in my company has changed dramatically as our firm has announced wave after wave of layoffs," John told me. "I've never felt particularly appreciated by the senior managers in my department. However, lately I'm beginning to consider them so unapproachable that the situation borders on being unprofessional. The only reason I'm not worried about my job is that they depend on me because I'm a good writer.

"Things came to a head recently over our annual report," John explained. "My firm has new management across the board. My boss, who is struggling with his own emotional reaction to our firm's re-organization, was anxious about how we would explain the firm's future strategy. When I suggested that we focus on connecting our efforts to rebuild the firm with the changes in our management team, he snapped at me. Later that day, we got a memo from senior management specifically telling us to discuss the management changes in the annual report for reasons that basically echoed my rebuilding suggestion. Rather than acknowledging my contribution, my boss grabbed credit for the idea himself and has been giving me the cold shoulder ever since. I know people act strangely under pressure, but this incident made me realize that I don't want to work in a company that doesn't value my insight anymore. The problem is, I don't want to go back to being a freelancer either — I have two kids and an ex-wife to support, and it's just too dicey. What scares me is that I'm not sure what I want to do anymore."

"How did you picture your authentic self as you did this exercise?" I asked him.

"As I wrote, I pictured a man who was valued by his team, who managed to find the time to stay in shape both physically and spiritually, and who was smiling because he had a happy relationship with the right woman," John told me.

"Did visualizing this ideal self give you any insights about the best response to your current challenges?"

"Some, but at this point these insights are more about how I'm

Our culture peculiarly honors the art of blaming, which it takes as the sign of virtue and intellect.

— Lionel Trilling

Everybody calls "clear" those ideas which have the same degree of confusion as his own.

— Marcel Proust

dealing with this problem on the inside rather than how I'm reacting on the outside. Reflecting on my authentic self helped me put into perspective the resentment I felt toward my boss for grabbing credit for my rebuilding idea. In fact, as I was writing from this perspective, I came up with a powerful financial metaphor for creativity. As I found myself writing, I came to the authentic understanding that 'ideas are like individual assets, and the ability to have them is like ongoing cash flow.' The more I thought about this, the more I realized that it doesn't matter who steals an idea from me. Okay — it makes me mad, and I'd prefer to avoid it, but it's not the end of the world. Having ideas stolen is going to happen from time to time in a competitive culture. What matters is the ability to keep generating great ideas in a changing environment. It's that creative flow that being in touch with my authentic self can help me tap."

"Sounds like your authentic self is a pretty good writer as well," I told him, smiling. "What were the top three priorities that came up for you when you were considering your life from the perspective of this self?"

"Being a good father to my children, owning a home of my own, and finding a stable romantic partner turned out to be my top three," he told me. "What surprised me as I did this was the realization that, right now, dealing with my financial concerns is more important to me than meeting the right woman. Fortunately, I remembered what you said about how our priorities shift based on our survival needs. I almost had a 'should attack' until I realized that there was nothing wrong with making managing my career my top priority during an economic downturn.

"As I worked through these questions, I was finally able to put that need to please my family by working for a big-name firm to rest without regret," John told me. "I realized that I could probably get even more financial security working for a medium-sized firm that would appreciate my contacts since I come from a big player. While money is important to me, it had been important to me for the wrong reasons. I

The greater the ignorance, the greater the dogmatism.

— Sir William Osler

Thou has commanded that an ill-regulated mind should be its own punishment.

— Saint Augustine

had reveled in making more money than my brother. I was allowing myself to be driven by sibling rivalry more than by financial necessity. Now that I'm conscious of this, I think I can let that desire go. I simply wasn't aware of the way it was influencing me and preventing me from seriously considering a position with a smaller organization."

The only way you can make a mistake with this exercise is if you answer it the way you feel you should. One of the main reasons that it is vital to weed out the shoulds is that these negative messages have the ring of internal commands rather than suggestions and keep us so rigidly focused on what we "should" become that we are no longer enjoying the process of getting there.

Shoulds are sneaky. Our psyches can fool us by allowing the rigid roles we play to mutate, so we may think we've gotten in touch with our true selves but all we've really done is switch masks at the costume ball of life. One of the key areas where some of the self-help systems fall down on the job is in preaching that all we have to do is think happy thoughts, and we will reconnect with our true selves while our troubles dissolve into the light. Promises like these are the philosophical equivalent of popping a pill to feel better so you don't have to learn from life's challenges. Both our negative and our positive feelings and experiences are vital parts of reality. Getting in touch with your authentic self will help you make good use of both the negative and the positive forces in your life in a gentle and transformative way.

Be mindful of dogmatic belief systems built on inflexible ideas of what is "good" and "bad." These types of beliefs work like Miracle-Gro on your shoulds. When well-intentioned people pursue a rigid interpretation of any personal-growth path, they can create a new set of shoulds that are every bit as limiting as those they started with. Clients following a list of spiritual shoulds come dragging into my office as

Mediocre minds usually dismiss anything which reaches beyond their own understanding.

— François Duc de La Rochefoucauld

We don't see things as they are, we see them as we are.

— Anaïs Nin

depleted of energy as any type-A agnostic. These rigid roles usually have people singing a rather robotic refrain along the lines of "I should be more spiritual...I should be more humble...I should work the twelve steps harder...I should get to synagogue more often" and so on. Now, don't get me wrong; I believe that religion and recovery programs can be wonderful sources of inspiration and support. However, when you pursue these paths from the perspective of your true self, you tend to create an inner song without as many shoulds in the refrain.

During my years as a portfolio manager, I battled a powerful list of shoulds as I contemplated leaving my career in finance to focus on my personal goals. I can remember taking an afternoon to research part-time social work programs in Boston, only to have my hopes dashed by the bureaucratic admissions professionals who insisted that there was no degree on the planet that could be pursued by someone trapped in my travel schedule. This really got me down because, after all, I "should" be able to do it all!

Even after I had focused on my goals enough to clarify my ambitions (I wanted to become what I desperately needed but couldn't find in those days — someone who had combined the skills of a licensed therapist with the perspective of a top business consultant), I found myself bombarded by a series of shoulds that threatened to paralyze me: You "should" maintain your earning power (anything can happen!). You "should" transition into an established profession, and so on.

I developed the previous exercise as I struggled to maintain my own professional momentum. As an experienced and tenacious businesswoman, I learned quickly that the challenge of dealing with my shoulds was every bit as real and as limiting as the challenge of finding an academic community that could give me the type of training I needed to make the professional transition I envisioned. Even after I had started on my new career path, I realized that if I didn't deal

People seem not to see that their opinion of the world is also a confession of character.

— Ralph Waldo Emerson

with the shoulds that were draining my energy and dampening my enthusiasm, I was going to lose focus on my goals and I wasn't going to succeed.

Many clients are eager to explore new ways to realize their professional potential. However, once they have started the coaching process, they quickly find out that one reason they have avoided clarifying their priorities is the risks they discover as they face changing their lives to reflect those priorities. Taking this leap is daunting for many people, because we live in a culture that has taught us that we "should" produce results quickly and effortlessly. We "should" make it look easy. And most important for many of us, we "should" stay safe.

To enjoy an authentically rewarding career, you will need to take meaningful risks on your own behalf. However, risk involves danger and the possibility of loss. The more we become hooked on pleasure and believe that success should come to us with "point-and-click" ease, the less we are able to deal with the emotional stress that taking risks entails. For many years, I struggled both personally and professionally to understand what really kept people from taking the risks necessary to create the lives they desired. In most cases, I found that what held people back could be summarized by one simple word: *fear*. Fear hides in our psyches by sneaking under a pile of shoulds.

This is not to say that many of the fears that come up when people are contemplating a career change aren't valid. It's simply terrifying to think about telling your boss that you want to be considered for a promotion in an environment where, if you don't get it, you may be knocked off the fast track permanently. It's downright scary to confront an aggressive co-worker who may undermine your popularity (not to mention your credibility!) with the other people in your department if you take a stand on difficult issues. It's absolutely gut-wrenching to consider leaving the security of a paid position, no matter how dysfunctional the work environment is, to consider following a professional dream that may pay off...and may not. These are all

The moment you find a technique, you become attached to it and there is no longer any open listening. The mind clings to methods because it finds safety in them. Real questioning has no methods, no knowing — just wondering freely, vulnerably, what it is that is actually happening inside and out. Not the word, not the idea of it, not the reaction to it, but the simple fact.

— Toni Packer

real fears; however, to move ahead professionally, we must be able to separate our real fears from our limiting beliefs.

One must be something to be able to do something.

— Goethe

The work you've done in the Awareness Stage has helped you to separate your genuine desires from the messages you have internalized from others about how you "should" proceed professionally. Now that you have completed this detective work, the next step is to cultivate the courage necessary to take meaningful risks on your own behalf. This is the work of the Emotional Ownership Stage.

STAGE II
EMOTIONAL
OWNERSHIP

I n the Emotional Ownership Stage you will begin to focus your entire being — your body as well as your mind — on achieving your professional goals.

Emotions are spontaneous reactions to situations that are triggered by memories and past conditioning. We experience emotions as physical sensations and mental pictures simultaneously. The shallow breathing that many of us experience when we are anxious to close a sale is a common physical response to tapping into general fears about financial survival. Similarly, many people notice that their jaws clench when their boss speaks to them in a disrespectful or abrupt tone. A clenched jaw is a common physical response to tapping into memories of anger that get stored in our bodies whenever we are treated disrespectfully.

When one is pretending, the entire body revolts.

— Anaïs Nin

In the Emotional Ownership Stage, you will build on your previous work in the Authentic Career Process by releasing your shoulds at an even deeper level. Most people know what they "should" do to enhance their professional success. Most people know that they "should" make strategic (and ethical) business decisions, present themselves with confidence, and react with grace under pressure. So why don't we all do these things? Why can't we just make a list of the top traits that help make us succeed, begin acting on these immediately, and get on with enjoying our success? Sadly, it's not that simple. This is because all of us devote a tremendous amount of energy to insulating ourselves from what we would prefer not to know about ourselves.

One of the most powerful ways that many people protect themselves is by numbing their bodies. Becoming aware of physical sensations, ranging from mild headaches to a general decline in stamina, is often the first step to uncovering vital information that they are suppressing. As one client told me, "I never seemed to be able to get a good night's sleep on Sunday. It took me a year and a half to realize that my body was screaming at me because I didn't feel fulfilled in my job anymore. Before that realization, I was doing everything from drinking warm milk to popping sedatives to shut my body down so it would obediently get the rest it needed to perform on the job. I ignored what my body was telling me because, for a long time, it was too terrifying to face the fact that I wasn't professionally fulfilled. This is because once I faced that, I knew I was going to have to take some risks to get my life back on track."

Our culture also supports a number of practices that help us to muffle our body's messages. Becoming overstimulated as we gaze at televisions that are installed everywhere from airports to elevators often keeps our minds rigidly focused on current events and distracted from the sensations in our bodies. Caffeine addiction has become a way of life for many workers that never get enough rest owing to a combination of workplace deadlines and lengthy commutes.

"So what if I am cut off from my body?" some exhausted and frightened clients have asked me. "I need a job, any job, and if I have to numb myself every night with a shot of whiskey and a video to keep going, who cares, as long as I make enough to retire and get out of the game?" For obvious reasons, this type of desperate challenge comes most frequently from clients who don't have families and children.

However, even if you have no greater priority in your life than personal success, cultivating your mind-body connection is vital to achieving your professional goals. This is because to be successful in a rapidly changing and competitive business environment, you must be able to see all sides of a complex question, not just the aspects that keep you in your emotional comfort zone. When you cut yourself off from the messages in your body, you are cutting yourself off from a flow of information and energy that can be vital to your success.

When we are in touch with our real desires and able to channel this energy toward our goals, there is almost nothing we can't achieve. To successfully focus our emotional energy, we must stay tuned in to our bodies. Getting in touch with the meaning behind the flow of

And I suppose that before I leave this world, one thing that I would wish for all the world to know, is that human contact is made by the connection of skin, eyes and voice tone. These are the things that are taught us before we had words. How our parents touched us, how they looked at us, what their voices sounded like, were all recorded in us.

—Virginia Satir

messages we receive from our bodies requires us to be more flexible about which feelings we will give ourselves permission to acknowledge.

Obviously, when you can't express your emotional reactions spontaneously, many great opportunities will pass you by. You may have a fabulous "gut instinct" about how your clients are going to react to your firm's latest ad campaign, but if you can't articulate your feelings spontaneously, you sit there like a mute until a few minutes later when someone else manages to articulate the same hunch and look like a hero.

Emotional rigidity is also one of the main reasons that many people become perpetual performers whose relationships become artificial and scripted. Many of us learn to play a role in life that not only reinforces the core beliefs of our family system but also serves to restrict our range of emotional experience. Sadly, when we play a part that guides us to ignore important emotions, uncomfortable feelings aren't eliminated — they are just repressed. Unmet personal needs frequently contribute to professional sabotage. Repressed feelings and desires can creep out in all the wrong places — from procrastinating about returning an important phone call to adopting an impatient tone with a co-worker or important client.

Getting passed over for promotion or losing a job are two things that inspire many people to reach out urgently for help. Frequently, however, people will only give themselves permission to receive "just enough" help to enable them to keep up appearances and bond with another system — *any* system — fast! The hope in such cases is that one can operate from a "slicker" version of the false self and get farther. Of course, if you continue to ignore the promptings of your authentic self, you are setting yourself up for burnout. *Burnout,* by the way, is a euphemism for depression, and when it strikes it robs people not only of their professional motivation but also of their zest for life.

However, long before burnout becomes a concern, long before business-related errors or interpersonal conflicts threaten an individual's track record, frequently there is an impressive history of physiological clues from migraines to digestive problems that, if acknowledged,

Before I built a wall
I'd ask to know what I was
walling in or walling out.

— Robert Frost

would have helped the person develop the emotional flexibility necessary to take positive action before the situation deteriorated.

Strengthening your mind-body connection helps you to build the foundation of inner emotional resilience that is vital to your success. As this connection strengthens, you are gradually able to identify your full range of feelings more spontaneously and to take fuller responsibility for your reactions to workplace challenges. This helps you make the transition from a life driven by your need to avoid uncomfortable situations to a life committed to resolving them.

The Emotional Ownership Stage will help you to work with your full range of emotional experience when facing professional challenges. This work also forms the foundation of emotional spontaneity you will need to proceed successfully to the next stage, Interaction. The work in this stage is divided into three chapters:

- *Chapter 4: "The Physical Foundation of Success."* The first goal of the Emotional Ownership Stage is to identify any physical sensations that stimulate thought patterns which in turn restrict your range of emotional experience. The work in this chapter is designed to help you explore the core beliefs that you hold onto to keep troubling emotions out of your conscious awareness. The goal is to help you learn to identify some of the physical responses that cue you to filter out unwanted feelings before you have consciously identified them.

- *Chapter 5: "Identifying Your Dominant Roles."* The second goal of the Emotional Ownership Stage is to identify the roles you have learned to play to keep uncomfortable feelings suppressed. This chapter begins by giving you a framework for understanding the way stressful situations may trigger you to exaggerate certain aspects of your personality as a way of avoiding unpleasant emotions. As your range of emotional awareness widens, you will be able to snap out of playing a restricting role when it no longer serves you, adopt the perspective of your authentic self, and adapt more spontaneously to professional challenges.

Outward security demands a high price: the acceptance of a continuous destruction of the personality.

— Ingmar Bergman

*The life I am trying to grasp
is the me that is trying
to grasp it.*

— R. D. Laing

- *Chapter 6: "Strengthening Your Authentic Self."* The third goal of this stage is to strengthen your connection with your authentic self. As you begin to trust your ideal self more fully, you will develop the ability to identify and manage the full spectrum of your emotional responses in any situation. One of the ways you strengthen this connection is by learning to clarify and trust your inner longings and tap into the power of your imagination. As you learn to trust yourself, you will be able to assume more responsibility both for your professional success and for the quality of your life in general.

Our bodies are the gatekeepers of the feelings we allow ourselves to experience and the memories we allow ourselves to access. A key challenge in reclaiming our full spectrum of emotional experience is that, for many of us, the inner gateway to our mind-body connection has been narrowed by a culture that has conditioned us to operate primarily on an intellectual level. An intellectually skewed perspective of reality ignores the emotional energy that infuses the ideas we internalize. It is important to identify this emotional energy whenever we can, because this is the energy that transforms ideas into core beliefs.

While the work in the Awareness Stage has helped you to gain an intellectual appreciation of how the core beliefs you internalized from your family may have influenced your professional effectiveness, this awareness is merely the first step in helping you to create a holistic strategy for achieving authentic success. Gaining an intellectual understanding of why your life and career are not working, without using this awareness as a foundation for making changes that will enhance your life, leaves you in the uncomfortable position of "suffering smart." You may be able to make scintillating conversation at a cocktail party about why your relationship with your father leaves you tongue-tied with authority figures, but this awareness alone will not prevent you from being passed over for promotion.

Emotional Ownership is the next step in building on the kind of mental awareness that can help you take your life and career to the next level. This awareness has begun in the minds of the scientific community who have tried to map the connection between ideas, feelings, and physical health. Groundbreaking work has been done throughout the medical community, such as the research done by the biophysicist Dr. Candice Pert, which explores the link between our physiology and our

CHAPTER 4

The Physical Foundation of Success

emotional experiences. Scientists have been researching the way we store memories at the cellular level. If we store memories in our bodies as well as our minds, then mental awareness only tackles the challenge of eliminating limiting beliefs from "above the neck."

We are operating above the neck whenever we assume that what we think is more important than what we feel. We are operating above the neck when we emphasize data over personal experience. We are operating above the neck when we deify logic and denigrate intuition. Many of us have learned to solve most of our problems intellectually. The work in the Emotional Ownership stage is about learning to use both your intellect and your emotions in a balanced way to achieve your professional goals.

The premise that you can't think your way out of a feeling is challenging for some. Many people who live "from the neck up" become confused about the energetic nature of feelings. Energy is neutral. It isn't good or bad — it just is. One of the most common sources of confusion about emotional energy is the idea that some feelings are superior to others. Emotional energy is not a moral issue. We can think of feelings as regulating the energy of an individual much like weather regulates the energy of our planet. Some people like thunderstorms, some people find them a little scary, but few would make the weather into a moral issue. Ideas such as "thunderstorms are bad" or "rain is bad, but sunshine is good" are obviously rather absurd.

From this perspective, it's easy to see how confused we can become when we have internalized beliefs such as "anger is bad." In a competitive world, we are going to feel anger. If we get caught up in the trap of judging our feelings, we will pretend we are experiencing the feelings we consider superior and suppress the ones we would prefer not to acknowledge.

Suppressed feelings that become stored in our bodies are part of our reality, whether we are comfortable experiencing them or not. What's more, when we ignore them for too long, these suppressed feelings can come bubbling up to the surface in a variety of inconvenient

My belief is in the blood and flesh as being wiser than the intellect. The body-unconscious is where life bubbles up in us. It is how we know that we are alive, alive to the depths of our souls and in touch somewhere with the vivid reaches of the cosmos.

— D. H. Lawrence

ways that can sabotage us. When people tell me things like "I don't know what came over me — I found myself sobbing in my boss's office before I could stop myself" or "I didn't really want to fire this guy, but I was so frustrated I didn't know what I was saying," they are often describing what happens when a flood of feelings that they have been trying to ignore finally breaks through.

We can't "think" our way out of the grip of limiting emotions any more than we can "think" of a way to get to our deeper levels of consciousness. Our connection with our authentic self comes from owning our truth. We own our truth as we get in touch with the physical sensations we experience when we tap the energy stored in our bodies. Thus, people who insist on functioning as if all their problems can be solved from the neck up never truly change the powerful pattern of physical sensations that can shape their behavior under pressure. Such individuals may temporarily change their style of interaction, but they are likely to revert to operating from their less conscious, more primal, and frequently limiting core beliefs when workplace challenges trigger them emotionally.

The emotional flexibility cultivated by doing the work in this chapter is vital in a rapidly changing economy, because professionalism counts most under pressure. When we are under pressure, our conscious mind frequently abdicates control to the deeper levels of knowing within us. It is at these deeper levels of consciousness that we are either proactive, in acknowledging the messages in our body, or reactive, in having our responses dictated by a flood of unexamined feelings.

In essence, your body can be thought of as an energetic warehouse. You can think of your emotional boundaries as the walls of this warehouse. When you draw your emotional boundaries too narrowly, you are squeezing out your potential for creativity, boxing in your intuition, and limiting the scope of your dreams. You are also cutting off your access to the power of your authentic self.

As you learn to tune in to your body, you give yourself permission to expand the walls of this warehouse, thereby letting in a wider range

Breath is the bridge which connects life to consciousness, which unites your body to your thoughts. Whenever your mind becomes scattered, use your breath as the means to take hold of your mind again.

— **Thich Nhat Hanh**

of emotional and physical sensations that may influence how you react in different situations. In the following exercise you will build on the work that you did in the Personal Tree of Life exercise with your feelings about the core beliefs you learned from your family.

When you did your Personal Tree of Life in chapter 1, you considered (perhaps for the first time) the systemic patterns you had inherited and internalized from your family. One thing that makes uncovering some of the most powerful systemic programming we internalize tricky is that every family system has its own rules about what is acceptable, appropriate, and relevant to discuss and what is best buried in a forgotten closet at the back of our psyches. As we go about uncovering the emotions that keep vital aspects of our family history less accessible to our conscious awareness, bear in mind that what we were not given permission to speak about in our families we frequently act out in our lives.

A body whose wisdom has never been honored does not easily trust.

— Marion Woodman

If anything is sacred, the human body is sacred.

— Walt Whitman

EXERCISE:

EXPANDING YOUR EMOTIONAL BOUNDARIES

The first part of this exercise involves reviewing your notes from your Personal Tree of Life work. You are going to need a large piece of paper that you can divide into two columns and a few uninterrupted hours to hunt for the missing clues that influence your internal programming.

Title one of the columns "Buried Feelings" and the other column "New Perspectives." Under the Buried Feelings column, list your responses to the following questions:

1. What was the most uncomfortable topic that I can remember discussing with my parents?
2. What physical sensations do I remember feeling when this topic came up?
3. What was the most uncomfortable topic that I can remember discussing with my siblings (and/or friends)?

4. What physical sensations do I remember feeling when this topic came up?

5. What challenging topics did my parents consider off-limits, and why?

6. How did my parents suppress feelings that came up around areas they didn't feel able to discuss?

7. How did my siblings (and/or friends) and I deal with feelings that came up around areas that were off-limits to open family discussion?

8. How did the rules in our family about what uncomfortable topics were off-limits affect my feelings toward and my relationship with my parents?

9. How did the rules in our family about what uncomfortable topics were off-limits affect my feelings toward and my relationship with my siblings (and/or friends)?

10. How did the rules in our family about what uncomfortable topics were off-limits affect the roles I have created in order to function successfully within my family system and my job today?

As you answer these questions, you may trigger the emotional responses you habitually experience when a situation is safe as opposed to when a situation presents danger. Bear in mind that the closer you get to core beliefs that have been buried for some time, the more mental and physical "fire walls" you have constructed to protect yourself from information you have been taught not to acknowledge.

Just to give you an example of how these fire walls can work, I have noticed that whenever a forbidden topic gets close to the threshold of a client's conscious awareness, he or she may become sleepy, suddenly remember an urgent phone call that has to be made, or find his or her mind just generally drifting away from the topic.

Most of us were trained not to discuss large parts of our childhood. Perhaps your saintly mother popped Valium to suppress the physiological sensations associated with the resentment she felt over an unfulfilling sex life. Perhaps your brother was diagnosed with

The body is a sacred garment. It's your first and last garment; it is what you enter life in and what you depart life with, and it should be treated with honor.

— **Martha Graham**

*We are linked by blood,
and blood is memory
without language.*

— Joyce Carol Oates

mental illness in his teens. Whatever the family secrets are, if they can't be openly discussed, the feelings go underground, and mental and physical fire walls get erected around them. The real problem is that when family secrets are buried in our psyches when we're children, we internalize our childlike interpretation of the situation as fact. This childlike perspective on the "facts" may or may not be accurate, but because it has never been openly discussed it will frequently become the foundation on which the individual bases his or her actions.

In the second column, which you have titled New Perspectives, write your responses to the following questions:

1. Who made the rules you have internalized that shape your personal code of conduct?
2. Which rules that you live by are helping you to succeed and grow, and which are holding you back?
3. Who do you believe is authorized to make rules of such a deep and defining nature? Your parents? God? Someone else?

Please take your time with the final questions in the New Perspectives column, because in these questions you are starting to get at information from your subconscious (or body) where you file memories and feelings that didn't get the family stamp of approval for open discussion.

*Only when you truly
inhabit your body can you
begin the healing journey.*

— Gabrielle Roth

4. What physical sensations do you experience when you disagree with the internalized voice of some "authority" making the rules that shape your perspective of reality?
5. What physical sensations do you experience when you disagree with parts of *yourself* over which rules need keeping and which you might do better without?
6. When you act in a way that takes you out of the role you internalized from your family system, what sensations do you experience in your body? Where do you feel them?
7. What do the physical sensations you experience when you question the rules you have internalized about how to behave tell you about yourself?

8. What do you usually choose to do with the information your body gives you when you consider an action that is out of your program?

Whether you store, file, or even bury an impression in your subconscious, you are creating an "energetic imprint" that shapes your ongoing sense of self. This exercise is designed to help you start getting your body involved in your change process. You see, your conscious mind may have been programmed not to remember a certain situation but your body registers everything — even what you choose to filter out of your mind.

Mindy, a pharmacist, came for coaching to deal with the anxiety she was feeling about returning to work after her honeymoon. A highly responsible professional, Mindy reported being so anxious and depressed that she was afraid she was going to make a mistake on a customer's prescription and not be able to keep up with the demands of her job. Mindy's experience doing the Expanding Your Emotional Boundaries exercise helped her listen to her body and identify a limiting belief that was eroding her quality of life and undermining her ability to do her job.

MINDY

"I never thought I'd find the right guy," Mindy confessed in one of our sessions. "I'd made so many sacrifices for my career that I figured having a reasonably secure job was all I could expect from life. Then I met Ted, and everything changed. He's adoring and fun-loving and has helped me experience joy for the first time in my life. My problem is that just when you'd think I would be able to relax and enjoy my life, I'm so stressed out that I'm afraid I'm sabotaging my career and my marriage.

When the spirit does not work with the hand there is no art.

— Leonardo da Vinci

I'm convinced that we must train not only the head, but the heart and the hand as well.

— Madam Chiang Kai-shek

Pity me that the heart is slow to learn, what the swift mind beholds at every turn.

— Edna St. Vincent Millay

There is a vitality, a life force, an energy, a quickening, that is translated through you into action, and because there is only one of you in all time, this expression is unique. And if you block it, it will never exist through any other medium and will be lost.

— Martha Graham

"I keep having these violent mood swings," Mindy lamented. "It wasn't until after my wedding that I realized how the violent mood swings that I have been dealing with in private for many years made it impossible to balance the anxiety I feel on the job with my desire to relax and enjoy my husband in our private time. My customers love me, but I'm constantly worried that I'm missing something and that I'm going to fail someone in some way. It's like I can never do enough."

It's important for clients to bear in mind that the quality of their personal and professional lives is always interrelated. You can't separate who you are as a person from who you are as a professional. "How are these mood swings affecting your marriage?" I asked her.

"The stress I feel at work can leave me so exhausted at the end of the day that I am prone to snap at Ted when I really don't want to," Mindy said sadly. "It's way beyond PMS. As a pharmacist, trust me, I've had my hormones checked. It's just a thousand little ways that I get anxious that other people are going to reject me."

"What physical sensations do you experience when you are feeling anxious?" I asked her, mindful of the fact that getting specific about these sensations is critical to success with this work.

"The most common one is that my breath gets shallow. Sometimes I also end up feeling drained of hope and exhausted. When this happens, I wind up blowing my diet by popping candy and getting a sugar rush so I can keep going," she confessed.

"Are there any specific problems on the job that trigger you?"

"When I was doing the exercise, I actually made a list of these," she told me. "A typical example is if an insurance company doesn't return my phone call within a few hours, I start imagining that the customer is going to hate me for not being more efficient. It can ruin my whole day. It can also ruin my whole night, because sometimes I can't shake the stress when I get home. I know this is ridiculous, but I don't want these self-esteem issues to spoil my relationship with my new husband or my career."

"Did doing this exercise help you identify any situations in your past that triggered this shallow breathing you described?" I asked her.

"I began experiencing that uncomfortable breathless feeling when I began trying to answer the question about issues my mom was uncomfortable discussing with me," Mindy began thoughtfully. "There's one main issue that my mom and I have always struggled with. In my late twenties, when I was at my grandmother's funeral, I had learned that my dad had actually been married to another woman when he met my mom — and that my mom believed that this other woman was really my dad's true love."

"Do you remember a specific physical sensation when you learned this secret?"

"Oh, yeah," Mindy said, shaking her head adamantly. "It felt like someone had unloaded a round of buckshot in my chest. Throughout my childhood, I had never suspected that either of my parents had been married before. It wasn't until one of my aunts got drunk and started babbling about my dad's first marriage that the secret came out. I was shocked that my parents could have kept something like this from me for so long.

"After this secret came out at the funeral, my mom started privately confessing to me that she was afraid my father had always loved this other woman and had never truly loved her. This was more information than I wanted from my mom, and it just made the fact that they had hidden this from me for so long even harder to bear.

"My chest kept getting tighter and tighter while I was doing this part of the exercise, and I had to remind myself to keep breathing," she told me.

It's important to do this particular exercise as thoughtfully and gently as possible. Getting the most from this exercise involves actually stopping as you work through the questions and taking the time to check in with the sensations you are experiencing as you mentally sort through your memories.

"When I got to the question of how my dad suppressed feelings he didn't know how to deal with, I remembered that when this secret

The sun shines not on us, but in us. The rivers flow not past, but through us, thrilling, tingling, vibrating every fiber and cell of the substance of our bodies, making them glide and sing.

— John Muir

came out, he had shown me a picture of his first wife," Mindy continued. "I was startled, because I looked a lot like her. Fortunately, there were never any questions in my mind about who my biological mother really was, because I had my birth certificate to prove that my mom was truly my mom, and all of that."

"Do you think there is a link between the tightness in your chest when you write about these memories and the tightness in your chest you are experiencing when you feel stressed at work?" I asked her.

"I've thought a lot about this, and I think the link is the nervous pressure I've always felt to keep my mom happy," Mindy told me. "I had known for years that she was angry at me about something, but I never knew what it was. I used to knock myself out to make great grades, keep my room clean, help around the house — anything to connect emotionally with her — but she was always cold and withdrawn. The tight feeling I get in my chest at work is the same tight feeling I got when I could never do enough to connect with my mother."

If you take the time to do this exercise thoughtfully, it can be very powerful work. It's vital that you take a break if necessary. If you are doing this on a weekend, you may want to go to the gym and come back to this work after you have worked out, or you may want to take a nap. If you're doing this on a weekday, you may want to jot down your insights and come back to this exercise later in the week.

"After a light snack, I came back to tackle the next section in the exercise," Mindy continued. "As I did the New Perspectives column, that pressure in my chest seemed to go away. Nothing I ever did seemed to be good enough for my mom. I remembered once when I confronted her because she would never come into my bedroom to talk with me. At times, it felt like she couldn't get far enough away from me. I told her, 'I make straight A's, I do everything right — what do you want from me?' My mom just looked at me coldly and told me, 'Mindy, you are so close to being perfect that I get frustrated when you're not.' I was devastated."

Mindy took a picture from her bag and handed it gently to me. "This is the photo my dad showed me of his first wife," she told me. "When I noticed how much I resembled the woman in this photo,

*The galaxies exist in you,
not printed as mere images
within your skull,
but in your every cell,
your every atom.*

— George Leonard

it hit me. My mom had been torn all these years between wanting to be a loving mother to me and the powerful mixed feelings of jealousy and fear she had suppressed because, in her mind, I looked like my dad's first wife. As I made this connection, something felt like it released in my chest, and I ended up crying for some time before I could finish the exercise. I realized that my mother wasn't ever really in competition with me. She loved me. My mother was in competition with another woman that she believed looked like me. That was why she was never truly close to me — and why I always felt like I could never do enough. That was why I was always so anxious that there was some hidden reason other people weren't going to like me — and why I was so anxious that I could never do enough.

"This exercise has helped me identify my limiting belief that 'I can never do enough.' It has also helped me identify the physiological trigger that lets me know I'm operating from this belief — a sensation of tightness in my chest that makes me feel like I can't breathe. Hopefully, as I learn to listen to my body more carefully, I can begin to slow down and do my job more thoughtfully and less anxiously. I'm going to work hard on releasing this limiting thought pattern so I can do my job without feeling drained and experience joy with my new husband."

If the dream says there is something wrong with your body, check. Long before you do, your body knows when something is wrong.

— **Marion Woodman**

Those who don't know how to weep with their whole heart, don't know how to laugh either.

— **Golda Meir**

Two important points from Mindy's victorious breakthrough with the Expanding Your Emotional Boundaries exercise are worth bearing in mind. First, what enabled Mindy to gain a valuable new perspective on her relationship with her mother came through her connection with her body. Mindy's ability to make the connection between her drive to keep "busy" and her desperate urge to distract herself from the pressure in her chest was an important breakthrough in freeing the blocked energy that had kept her locked in self-defeating patterns. Mindy stuck with her breathing when this exercise became emotionally painful, and she refused to duck the challenge by letting her intellect take over.

Often it takes more than one kind of work to make this type of perceptual breakthrough. If you've been in traditional therapy for some time and you don't seem to be making significant progress, perhaps it's time to try some kind of bodywork, such as acupuncture, Alexander Technique, massage, and so on. We all need to try new approaches to personal growth over time to keep challenging ourselves emotionally and intellectually.

Second, Mindy made the effort to do this exercise carefully. I believe that you get out of the Authentic Career Process what you put into it. My clients who actually do the exercises assigned to them between sessions make significantly more progress than those who allow their minds to "filter out" the homework suggestions from week to week.

The Expanding Your Emotional Boundaries exercise draws from my personal experience as well as from my professional experience with clients. Before I made the transition from portfolio management to coaching, I learned the importance of working with a variety of self-exploration methods to keep moving forward. I was writing in my journal by the river one afternoon during a vacation week that I was spending at a spa in Austin, Texas. As I wrote, I realized that the emotional inertia I was experiencing in my traditional therapy was impeding my progress in a way I never would have accepted professionally. As I continued to write, I reflected on the fact that for the past two years my therapy had boiled down to recycling the same tired litany of complaints over the lack of fulfillment I felt in my job and the lack of passion I experienced in my personal life. Not only was this getting boring, I was beginning to become concerned that I was reinforcing the negative energy of these complaints by droning on about them week after week without making any fresh discoveries.

My lazy afternoon of journaling by the river turned into a type of prayer. I found myself wondering, half-consciously, what I could possibly do to move beyond the wall I had hit in my therapy and do the emotional work necessary to take my life to the next level.

The lively world of our emotions, fears and responses is like a great forest with its fauna. We experience those feelings as though they were wild animals bolting through the foliage of our thinking being, timidly peering out in alarm or slyly slinking and cunningly stalking, linking us to our unknown selves.

— Paul Shepard

I had scheduled a massage after dinner at the last minute, so I ended up getting a young woman who was a massage student rather than one of the more experienced staff members. This woman shyly informed me that she wasn't sure what I wanted, but that if I'd let her know what I liked she'd do her best. Rather than starting in a traditional manner, she began working on one of my knees. Suddenly, I found myself erupting in tears and experiencing a flood of mental pictures and feelings reflecting the frustration I felt about feeling trapped in a relationship and a professional role that were both suppressing my creativity.

When I started crying, the massage therapist stopped anxiously and asked me if I was all right. Through my tears, I asked her to keep working on the same spot as long as my emotional reaction didn't make her uncomfortable. She pressed on — and so did I. This woman and I met for lunch the next day to talk about what had happened. We were both stunned by the level of emotional and energetic release that took place during our hour together. She told me that she had been in therapy herself for many years trying to clear some of the same limiting emotions that I was struggling with. When I asked her why she'd started working on my knee that night, all she could tell me was, "I've never done that before — it just seemed right at the time."

This massage therapist and I worked together every night for the rest of my stay in Austin. She would massage certain parts of my body, and I would allow whatever pictures and feelings this brought up for me to flow as freely as I could give myself permission to do. What we both discovered through this process is that working with the body is vital to releasing the emotional charge associated with deeply held feelings and beliefs.

Over the years, I have maintained a friendship and a professional collaboration with this woman in Austin as well as with a wide variety of other talented people involved in exploring the role that the body plays in our emotional and spiritual evolution. The feedback I've received from many of these talented professionals has contributed to

The body is the shore on the ocean of being.

— Sufi (anonymous)

No matter where we are, the shadow that trots behind us is definitely four-footed.

— Clarissa Pinkola Estés

*The images we take in
are the nutrients of
our subtle body.*

— Marion Woodman

the creation of exercises such as Expanding Your Emotional Boundaries. The collaborative work I continue to do with colleagues who specialize in bodywork continues to reinforce my conviction that to achieve meaningful change, we must involve all aspects of our being in the process. This means we must focus our minds, our bodies, and our spirits simultaneously on achieving our authentic goals.

In the last chapter, you focused on the physiological sensations that are triggered when you operate from a limiting core belief. In this chapter, you are going to focus on the way the roles you play can restrict your range of emotional experience.

Many of us have become performers to survive in competitive work environments. However, playing a role is a shaky long-term strategy. Eventually, something's got to give. You can only restrain your natural impulses for so long, and then eventually those pesky desires and creative impulses are going to force their way to the surface. If you don't spot the clues that your authentic self gives you, you may find that your career is not progressing and that you are on your way to burnout.

Emotional rigidity is the major cause of burnout today. It's sometimes tough to spot the motivational deterioration that leads to burnout, because most veterans of a competitive workplace have learned to keep problems well hidden — especially from themselves. Things usually have to unravel on the outside before many people realize that something's wrong. However, at some point a person who has suppressed unwanted feelings will no longer be able to maintain the emotionally costly fiction that everything is fine and will begin to manifest problems that can no longer be ignored.

The problem is, most people have been playing their assigned roles so obediently for so long that they don't even realize they are playing a part. After all, if you are truly unaware of the full range of your emotions, how would you know if you were only accessing part of them?

The work in this second chapter of the Emotional Ownership Stage is designed to help you understand the way that a certain cycle

CHAPTER 5

Identifying Your Dominant Roles

of energy can work either to reinforce your commitment to playing a role or to help you tap into the broader perspective of your authentic self. Below I will discuss how this cycle works.

WHEN THE CYCLE REINFORCES THE ROLE

Sometimes it seems as if some kind of "psychic software" is programming people to respond in certain ways. This programming actually loops just like computer code does, creating a self-reinforcing cycle of interaction between an individual and their company. My interpretation of the way this cycle of self-reinforcing rigidity affects us is as follows.

1. The Cycle Begins: The role gets triggered because the individual's focus is on external approval from superiors rather than on internal satisfaction. He or she may subordinate authentic impulses to please others in the organization.

To grasp the way this cycle works more fully, let's consider Sally's experience. Sally, who had recently finished her MBA and joined a consulting firm, found that she and her fellow associates were constantly worried that they would lose their jobs because their company was downsizing. "People who used to be friends at school before joining this organization now barely acknowledge each other in the halls," she told me. "People get fired all the time here, and we all have to go on working like we never knew or even cared about the latest group who lost their jobs. The emotional climate is so intense that I have to flood my body with caffeine to suppress the feelings of dread I wake up with on Monday morning when I have to force myself to show up. I feel like I have to play the role of this hyperefficient, emotionless executive at this job, or I'll be singled out as being too 'soft' to make it in this place. Nobody ever says this — in fact there's a great deal of lip service paid to being a team member, but it's all hype. In reality, most of us are so scared of losing our jobs when we know it's going to be tough to find another one that we are driven to play our parts out of fear."

It is more difficult to be a complete human being than a saint. It means nothing can be excluded or suppressed.

— Steven Levine

2. The Role Gets Reinforced: Feelings of victimization often produce a series of physiological responses that are related to memories of situations when the individual was not appreciated in his or her family. These physical sensations compel the person to act in accordance with the role.

"I ask myself every morning how long I can stay in this tense work environment," Sally told me. "When I joined this firm, I was told that I was going to be groomed to run an important division in our department. Now they've fired several of the associates they hired with my class, and they've got me doing thankless administrative work for a group of overworked senior associates who are snapping at me all the time. Sometimes I get this sick feeling in the pit of my stomach that I know is a signal from my body that this isn't a great place for me long-term. It reminds me of the feeling I used to get when I wanted to talk something important out with my mom, but she just got all busy and officious to avoid dealing with me. This feeling is a huge red flag that I'm not being appreciated in this environment. Some days this feeling is so powerful I just want to walk out of this job and not look back. However, I know that if I quit I need to do it in a way that doesn't burn my bridges in the business community — and I need to have a plan in place for what I want to do next. What happens to me most days when my stomach starts to churn is that I realize that I'm so scared about building the track record I'm going to need to make my next move that I simply force myself to ignore my feelings and go on playing my part."

3. Feelings Get Fragmented: Powerful mood swings and even acts of professional sabotage or mean-spirited behavior may occur sporadically when a person feels trapped into behaving according to the rigid script of the professional role.

"I knew something was going to have to change when I caught myself screaming at one of my colleagues one evening because we needed to get a presentation out for one of the senior partners, and the printer broke. I was unloading on this guy who sat near the main printer because we had been having trouble with this machine for weeks, but he hadn't bothered to call a repair person or take any action

When the fight begins within himself, man is worth something.

— Robert Browning

The images of the unconscious place a great responsibility on a man. Failure to understand them, or a shrinking of ethical responsibility, deprives him of his wholeness and imposes a painful fragmentariness on his life.

— Carl Jung

to head off the problem before we had a crisis on our hands. When I got home and calmed down that evening, I realized that I'd been unreasonable. This guy just sat near the printer — he wasn't responsible for its maintenance. However, I was so terrified that somebody was going to blame me for the presentation being late that I found myself publicly blaming someone else before anyone could point the finger at me. Now this guys thinks I'm a monster, and I'm earning a reputation as one of those psycho people that nobody will ever want as their manager. What kills me about this is that this isn't who I really am. I've always felt that my ability to motivate others and be a fair person were some of my greatest skills. I realize that I'm so driven by fear these days that the role that's taking over in the workplace is less and less a reflection of who I truly am."

4. The Role Gets Reaffirmed, and the Cycle Begins Again: Fear of losing status in the organization forces the individual to frantically seek ways to gain the approval of others in the hierarchy to prevent buried feelings from further jeopardizing his or her status. This frantic search for approval causes the person's psyche to become even more powerfully imprinted by the role, and the cycle begins again.

"I found myself trapped in a no-win situation where being straightforward about what was happening in our department just didn't seem to be a viable option," Sally lamented. "The senior associate was outraged that we missed the deadline for this presentation, which didn't surprise me, because everyone in our department is seething with resentment these days. It doesn't take much to set off any of us. What senior management honestly needs to know is that so many people have been fired in our group that everyone is trying to do the work of five people and important things are constantly slipping through the cracks. However, when I was confronted with the blind rage of this senior associate, I found myself too intimidated to give him the bigger picture. Instead, I told him that I had been nagging people in our department to fix the printer for weeks and that nobody had listened to me. This was bull, but it enabled me to deflect his anger onto someone else and hang on to my job. Now I'm afraid that although I may keep my job, I'm going to be responsible for someone else losing his position. My stomach has been so upset that I have to have a giant bottle of antacid in my desk drawer just to get through the day. This situation has been really hard on my self-esteem. I feel caught in a vicious circle where the more I compromise my values, the harder it gets to be to speak my own truth."

WHEN THE CYCLE REINFORCES THE AUTHENTIC SELF

1. The Cycle Begins: Because the individual is able to tap into the natural instincts and creative inspiration of the authentic self, he or she is then able to interact with others in a way that is both creative and nonthreatening.

As Sally began to cultivate her mind-body connection, she learned to see things more from the perspective of her ideal self. This helped her draw on her interpersonal skills in a way that furthered her own ambitions as well as the organization's goals. "In business school, I'd learned to think myself out of complicated situations. However, nobody had prepared me for the primal emotions of fear and rage that were enveloping everyone in our department. As I began trying to tune in to the physical sensations I was experiencing, instead of popping another antacid to shut my body up, I realized that my gut was screaming at me whenever there were powerful emotional currents swirling around in a situation that we were all trying to ignore by keeping busy. Instead of throwing myself into the latest task to block out the angry and resentful stares of my colleagues, I started asking nonthreatening questions like, 'Am I missing something here? Is there anything else you need to tell me?' At first people were pretty guarded about being frank with me. However, I managed to clear the air with a few key people in my department who admitted that they didn't think they could trust me. This was a beginning. Frankly, I couldn't blame them; it had gotten to the point where my behavior was so fear driven that I didn't feel like I could trust myself. However, listening to my body began to give me a simple but valuable indicator that there

> *I never really address myself to any image anybody has of me. That's like fighting with ghosts.*
>
> — Sally Field

was something happening in a situation that my adrenaline-driven mind hadn't grasped. As I learned to become more conscious of the emotional responses of the people I worked with, I began to realize that listening carefully to other people is one of the most nurturing things anyone can do in a tense corporate environment. I also realized that, when everyone's terrified, listening is the first skill that seems to evaporate."

2. The Authentic Self Gets Reinforced: As the individual learns to see more from the perspective of the authentic self, he or she experiences a surge of personal power that is both physiological and psychological.

"I was really surprised by the increase in my energy level after I'd been heeding my body's signals for a while," Sally admitted. "I had no idea how draining it had been for my mind to be constantly focusing on dramatic scenarios to distract me from the subtler emotional dynamics that my body managed to sense. The emotional environment of our department was saturated with tense questions such as, Who's having a turf war with whom? Who's a rising star? Who's washed up? The drama was so riveting it's amazing we got any work done. What's more, when the competition heated up, it seemed like even the most independent-minded people in our group felt forced to narrow their focus to their personal advantage. For most of us, this didn't feel like self-absorbed behavior when the heat was on — it felt like survival. In truth, at times it was. The amazing part of strengthening my mind-body connection was that suddenly I realized that a whole world of emotional information was influencing everyone's performance. Our productivity wasn't just driven by the numbers in the reports we sold to our customers; it was also made up of the network of hopes and dreams that held our tense organization together. Becoming more conscious of the cues in my body gave me a kind of shorthand for knowing when I needed more information about what my colleagues and clients were feeling — not just about what they were thinking. One cue I learned to spot consistently was that I seemed to get the same uncomfortable feeling in my stomach when

The reason we are united in the spirit to both heaven and hell is to keep us in freedom.

— Emanuel Swedenborg

Nothing determines who we will become so much as those things we choose to ignore.

— Sandor McNab

my colleagues weren't telling me about their frustrations that I did as a kid when my mother would start to get silently resentful about the amount of energy it took to look after me and my sisters. This physical clue has improved my job performance in many ways. First, paying attention to the sensations in my body has helped me start to ask more insightful questions in staff meetings. Second, listening to my body reminds me to take the time to connect emotionally with my colleagues — this has already helped me rebuild my relationships with several people in my department. Most important, tuning in to my body has helped me start to rebuild my relationship with myself. This has given me the self-confidence to believe that I can survive in this job without having to do so at the expense of those around me. What's more, I'm sleeping better, and I've stopped popping antacid pills like they were a food group."

3. Feelings and Desires Become Harmonized: Eventually, the individual's ability to maintain healthy professional alliances and pursue profitable opportunities under pressure contributes to his or her gaining the confidence of senior management.

"As I began to feel more self-confident, I became less invested in whether I was getting attention from senior management all the time. While I've always wanted to think of myself as a woman who is more interested in doing the job well than in self-promotion, it wasn't until I was calmer on the inside that I was able to be objective about how much of my energy had been spent performing for those above me — and how little had been directed toward actually doing the task at hand. The fascinating thing was that once I truly let go of the need to play my role constantly, I started getting recognition in ways I hadn't dreamed of before. For example, one of the senior associates was staffing for a big client project where I had hoped to be included on the team. When the memo came out, I hadn't been selected. To my own amazement, I didn't care. In the past, this is just the type of thing that would have plunged me into an internal abyss of self-pity and had me dialing compulsively for the first friend I could share my rage with.

*Out of perfection,
nothing can be made.
Every process involves
breaking something up.
The earth must be broken
to bring forth life.
If the seed does not die,
there is no plant.
Bread results from the
death of wheat.*

— Joseph Campbell

Grace strikes us when
we are in great pain
and restlessness. . . .
Sometimes at that
moment a wave of light
breaks into our darkness,
and it is as though a
voice were saying:
"You are accepted."

— **Paul Tillich**

I wasn't pretending not to care or acting mature, I really didn't care. The real test of my response came when I was caught in the hall by some colleagues that night who were confident that they could get me to start ranting about how unfair our team selection was. In the past, I would have been an easy mark for a juicy gripe session — complaining used to make me feel alive. However, I actually found myself reassuring these people that there would be plenty of opportunity for us to add value behind the scenes. My colleagues teased me for a bit, but they were as surprised as I was when they realized I wasn't faking it — I really wasn't upset! Somehow, the ever-present grapevine must have gotten a replay of this scene to my boss's boss (you simply can't keep a secret in our office!), because he called me in later that week to tell me how much he appreciated my professional attitude. What's more, he let me know that he was putting me on a project where I would be helping him deal with one of our firm's most important accounts."

4. *The Authentic Self Gets Reaffirmed, and the Cycle Begins Again: As the individual becomes even more adept at trusting his or her natural instincts, he or she is given more freedom for creative expression and continues to mature as a professional.*

"I'm learning quickly that trusting my gut is one of the most important skills I bring to my work as a consultant," Sally told me later in our work. "I've developed a great relationship with one of our firm's most important clients by paying attention to how this client feels about his business — not just what the latest numbers are reflecting. Some of our clients are founders of some amazingly successful companies. I've had long talks with some of the senior partners in our firm about the role that the personal evolution of these people has had on their professional decisions. I frequently tell people that I'm 'going on my gut' or following my intuition, and the people in my firm take my recommendations very seriously when I phrase it this way. The senior partners frequently ask me what my intuition is telling me about a tricky situation. I'm developing a reputation for being a valuable strategic asset in our firm because of my 'sophisticated' understanding of human dynamics in business. What am I really doing? Just paying attention to what my body is telling me as simply and honestly as I can."

Now, I'm sure that all of you who have done your exercises up to this point realize that the tricky part of this cycle is that most people don't realize it is going on. When we wake up to our authentic selves, we realize that we can do something that the computers still can't — we can reprogram ourselves. Once you become more conscious of this process, the gig is up. The next exercise is intended to help you "upgrade your software" so that you are reinforcing a new cycle of behavioral interaction with others.

The best way out is always through.

— Robert Frost

EXERCISE:

THE CYCLE OF THE ROLE AND THE CYCLE OF THE AUTHENTIC SELF

Remember a professional challenge in which you played the role you have learned to adopt to be successful. As you reflect on this memory, consider the cycle of the role, as discussed above, and write about any aspects of your memory that may coincide with the various stages of the cycle of that role.

After you have done this, imagine how you might have handled this same situation from the perspective of your authentic self. Reflect on this memory again, but this time go through the various stages of the cycle of the authentic self and write out in detail how you might have responded to this same challenge from this more integrated perspective of reality.

Finally, write your reflections on the key differences between the ways you responded playing your role versus being your authentic self. Note any key physiological or mental cues that may help you tackle future challenges from a more authentic perspective.

The old skin has to be shed before the new one can come.

— Joseph Campbell

Peter is a young investment advisor who just joined a money management firm. He found this exercise helpful in understanding how he could handle his new boss at their weekly investment meetings.

PETER

"My boss, Andy, is always interrogating me about any detail he can find that may make me look unprepared with my investment positions. It's not that he singles me out so much — he does this to everyone. It's just that I get so worked up when the spotlight is on me that I seem to trip over myself."

"How does the role you slip into at work affect your sense of self in this situation?" I asked him.

Very great rivers flow underground.

— Leonardo da Vinci

"No matter how well prepared I am for our weekly investment meeting, I always feel slightly nauseated and like a little kid being sent to the principal's office. The more I try to suppress these feelings, the more worked up I get. The more I thought about the self-defeating role I was playing, the more I realized that I was actually putting myself down far more harshly than Andy could ever do. I realized I was literally psyching myself out by saying things to myself like, 'You're a fake, and they're going to expose you. You don't deserve to be here — and they know it.'

"It got to the point during a particularly bad period where I was drinking heavily the night before our weekly investment meetings, and the stress I was feeling was beginning to come out in the way I responded to my wife and kids," Peter confessed.

Suppressing powerful feelings required to operate from a role can be so emotionally draining that it creates a craving for relief. For many clients, if the role they play becomes extremely rigid or self-defeating, this craving may erupt into cycles of addictive behavior, ranging from overeating and compulsive spending to drug abuse.

"My fear of being raked over the coals had caused me to blame other people in our department for oversights whenever Andy caught them — even when they were my fault," Peter confessed as he looked at the floor. "I'm really ashamed when I think about this, but I couldn't seem to take the blame for anything that went wrong because I was so afraid of losing points with the guys who had been there longer than I had.

"When my guilt and insecurity got the better of me, I found myself hanging around the office after hours like a puppy dog. When I began to realize that I hadn't behaved like a very nice guy toward some of my colleagues, I wanted to act like a nice guy, hoping people wouldn't start to secretly hate me. I was trying to make conversation with Andy and some of the other guys — anything to get an external sign of their approval."

One of the most frequent insights that clients report gaining from doing this exercise is that the approval of others ultimately doesn't count for much if they don't approve of their own behavior. When people start to consider what they would do if they were behaving in a way that reflects their ideal self, they are able to envision taking action from a position of inner confidence where their ethical values and the financial values of their corporate culture are not mutually exclusive. "What happened when you considered how you would handle this situation if you were operating more from the perspective of your authentic self?" I asked him.

"I knew my authentic self would realize that I was smart, that I'd done the best research work I could on my investment positions, and that if Andy and the group didn't agree with me, that was their choice," Peter began thoughtfully. "I felt a surge of inner strength when I imagined myself actually looking Andy in the eye when he spotted something that I had missed and saying, 'Thanks — that's helpful.'

"I also realized that the next time Andy tried to make it personal and just got enraged because I'd missed some detail, I was going to ask to meet with him privately after the meeting. I guess I have to come to terms with why he's angry with me and inspire his trust. To do this, I also have to rebuild my trust in myself. I never would have come to this conclusion without doing all these exercises. For a long time, I couldn't even admit to myself how out of line my behavior had gotten because I was anxious about losing status. Now that I get this, it feels much easier to confront him."

God, give us grace to accept with serenity the things that cannot be changed, courage to change the things which should be changed, and the wisdom to distinguish the one from the other.

— **Reinhold Niebuhr**

"Did this exercise help you focus on changing how you react to other people at your office?" I asked.

"I've made a decision to ease up on seeking Andy out so much after hours," Peter told me. "I know there is a problem in our relationship, and we are going to have a frank talk about it. However, I'm also conveying my insecurity by running after him like a scared puppy. I'm going to wait and see how long it takes him to come to me. That will be interesting."

The act of visualizing how their authentic self would behave, from maintaining eye contact to speaking in a more courageous vocal tone, is so powerful that many people find that even imagining doing this exercise reinforces their self-esteem. The self-esteem boost that comes from this work helps people recommit to operating according to their higher values and ideals under pressure. It also helps reinforce the foundation of emotional resilience people need to remain productive and act with professionalism under pressure. "Did this exercise help you see yourself differently?" I asked him.

"I have a lot to offer my investment group professionally," Peter replied, some pride creeping into his voice. "I know I'd be gone if they didn't realize this. The next time I hear that litany of 'You're a fake' starting in my head, I'm going to correct this. I'm not a fake. I'm just a guy whose got some rebuilding to do."

Peter's experience with this exercise brings to light an important point. You may uncover many limiting thoughts as you work through this process. Many people express despair when they initially become conscious of how negative they have been with themselves. The good news? You're not responsible for your first thought. Your first thought may come from old programming and may pop into your mind before you know what hit you. However, *you are responsible for your second thought.* Once you catch yourself falling into a self-limiting internal dialogue, that is your cue to correct your thinking. This is how you learn, over time, to get off the treadmill of the role and ride the waves of energy produced by your authentic self as you grow and change.

EXERCISE:

CUEING THE ROLE

This exercise builds on the work you did in the previous exercise to reinforce your ability to respond consciously (as opposed to reacting unconsciously) to workplace challenges. It is designed to help you clarify the perspective that you have internalized as a result of playing your role so brilliantly for so long. Please take your time with this, and be gentle with yourself. Remember that the roles we play aren't "bad"; they are just based on limited information.

Assassination is the extreme form of censorship.

— George Bernard Shaw

Keeping in mind your new understanding both of the role you play with your professional colleagues and of the perspective you have gained about how your past programming has reinforced this role, record your answers to the following questions:

1. What types of experiences give you a sense of accomplishment when you are successfully playing your professional role as you define it? When you are being your authentic self?

2. What physical sensations do you associate with a sense of accomplishment from the perspective of your role? From the perspective of your authentic self?

3. How do you view the actions of others from the perspective of your role? From the perspective of your authentic self?

4. How does your current work environment enhance or hinder your ability to play your role?

5. How does your current work environment enhance or hinder your ability to be your authentic self?

6. What are the "rules of life" that your professional role operates by, and how do these rules shape your definition of success? What are the "rules of life" according to your authentic self?

The goal here is to help you define as clearly as possible the role you play in order to function well professionally. There is no right or wrong here — this is simply an exploratory exercise to help you clarify your perspective of reality. Being clear about the distinction between the drives associated with your role and the desires of your authentic self is critical, because the most effective strategy in the world can't move you forward if you are unclear about your destination.

While many people complete this exercise in one or two nights, please go gently. Emotionally, this is one of the toughest exercises in the Authentic Career Process. Mindy, the pharmacist who experienced such a dramatic reaction to the Expanding Your Emotional Boundaries exercise, avoided this one for several weeks. Her main gambits for putting off this stage of the work were either to thank me for how much the previous exercise had helped her, thus subtly suggesting that she felt her internal work was completed, or to fill our coaching time with a dramatic recitation of the workplace drama du jour. I mention this to emphasize that it is natural to slow down in the Emotional Ownership Stage and that your psyche may come up with some slick ways to justify pulling back.

Being gentle with yourself when you need to slow down must be balanced against the knowledge that the closer you get to a real breakthrough, the more the internalized voices of your programmed role delight in throwing you off the scent by cheerfully reassuring you that you are "done."

Mindy was clearly on the threshold of reconnecting with her authentic self, but the toughest part of the work was yet to come as she approached her work with Cueing the Role.

MINDY

"I was shocked by my response to this exercise," Mindy confessed. "It's not like I haven't gotten a great deal out of the other work you have encouraged me to do, but I realized suddenly that I was enraged with you! 'Who is this psycho-coach telling me how important it is to get in touch with myself *anyway?*' I found myself fuming. 'I don't need this! I have a great job and a great husband — who *cares* if I have the odd mood swing! I don't! I quit!' My body was flooded with adrenaline, and I was enraged at the prospect of doing this work. Then, at just about the moment I was ready to dial you and leave a syrupy-sweet message about appreciating our work but no longer needing your services, my husband, Ted, walked in. He asked me what was wrong, and I showed him the exercise and suddenly, out of nowhere, my frustration erupted, and I started crying. Ted listened to me spew venom about how stupid it was for me to let you upset my peace of mind by stirring up all this emotional stuff when my real goal was to keep earning my salary and get ahead.

"I figured he'd be sympathetic because, after all, he's a man, and they generally hate all that touchy-feely stuff. I was very surprised when, after my tirade wound down, Ted mentioned quietly that it was interesting that I was having such a strong reaction to what looked like a pretty simple list of questions to him. He gave me a hug and suggested that I at least finish this last exercise before I wrote coaching off. He told me he'd make dinner for the two of us so I'd have something to look forward to when I was done. I was stunned. Here was my virile husband being emotionally available while I was reacting like the worst caricature of patriarchal defensiveness on the planet! I felt surrounded. He was encouraging me . . . you were encouraging me . . . so I went for it on blind faith."

Mindy's reaction to this exercise may sound dramatic, but I have found that many clients report feelings such as resentment, frustration, and even fear as they uncover the personal sacrifices they have made to fit in or please others in the course of their careers. These powerful feelings can create an emotional backlash that, if ignored, can cause people to abandon their attempts at achieving success on their own terms because the emotional toll seems too daunting. However, for clients who are able to hang in there, the payoff is life changing.

I have known shadow, and I have known sun; and now I know these two are one.

— **Rudyard Kipling**

Rudeness is the weak man's imitation of strength.

— Eric Hoffer

"At first, I started just writing out clipped answers to these questions in angry little choppy sentences. I didn't like feeling cornered. Then, as I read through the questions, I suddenly realized that it was the *role* I play that was feeling cornered — and that this was only part of me. What's more, it was the *role* that had been fueling the adrenaline rush of anger in my body that had almost derailed me from doing this exercise. I grabbed the favorite picture of myself as a child that I'd used in the "Personal Tree of Life" exercise and I went out to retrieve the CD I'd played while I'd been doing it. Ted smiled at me from the kitchen as I headed back into the bedroom. I was feeling more than a little sheepish at this point.

"As I was reflecting on how I got a sense of accomplishment from my professional role, I got this hideous image in my mind's eye of myself dressed in my lab coat, smiling — but with no life in my eyes and no joy in my heart. That smile was coming from fear.

"I realized that my powerful avoidance of this exercise came from the realization that the nightmare that I would become a workaholic robot might leave me feeling disoriented and terrified," Mindy continued softly. "What's worse, a wave of self-loathing washed over me as I began to flash on the thousands of tiny ways I had given my power away to please others over the years. I had smiled obediently when I'd wanted to scream in the face of uncaring insurance representatives and demanding clients. I had undermined other women whom I was supposed to train to help me deal with customers (my envious mother had taught me to fear women in general), and I had rushed through the best years of my life in a frenzy of hyperactivity to distract myself from the murderous rage seething just below the surface of my consciousness. No wonder I was avoiding the physical sensations associated with this — the whole realization left me nauseated! This wasn't pretty. My professional armor was coming off and, underneath, I felt like a lobster without a shell."

It's important for clients to bear in mind that no matter how painful the images that they uncover doing this work are, these images are not new to them. I remind every client who does this exercise that they have been operating with these inner images and beliefs for years, and that the only new part is that they are now becoming more conscious of their inner world. Also, for every image of pain and vulnerability that we hold, there is always an offsetting image of strength inside us to keep us centered as we grow.

"I kept finding my eyes wandering to a photograph of myself as a little girl," Mindy told me. "I was smiling up at the sun, my arms raised toward the sky and my hair blowing free in the wind. As I was looking at this picture, suddenly I got the most powerful hit of self-respect I can remember. My body flooded with a sense of peaceful power that felt like psychic champagne. I realized that I had survived myself. I had survived my own best efforts to demean myself, to minimize my talents, and even to ignore the longings of my soul.

"Suddenly I felt powerful rather than powerless about taking the time alone to do this work. The litany of internal command — 'just do this fast and get it over with!...stop wasting time on personal growth and make some money!...this is no time for you to be fiddling around with your feelings'— began to get fainter and fainter as I continued to work. I genuinely had to give myself credit. Under the layers of rationalizations, half-truths, and tense compromises, my true self was still there. In spite of the best efforts of the medical school and all the systems that had trained me, I was still committed to being myself. In that moment I realized that if I could survive myself, I could survive anything. I was finding my way home to my true self.

"The rest of the exercise fell into place after that. My authentic self loved people — my role was terrified of being exposed as a fake. My role whirred through life in an intellectual panic — my true self was amazingly serene about time. My role was revered for taking care of endless emergencies with robotic precision — my authentic self was more interested in helping people heal. Ever since I could remember, all my authentic self had wanted was to matter. That night, I realized

Everybody wants to be somebody;
nobody wants to grow.

— Goethe

that nothing I did in my career was going to make me matter if I didn't matter to myself."

As I said above, Cueing the Role is one of the toughest exercises in the Authentic Career Process. This is because people who are courageous enough to confront the dominant role they may have played professionally frequently discover that they cannot integrate the fractured pieces of their self without acknowledging the ways they have "sold" the most precious aspects of themselves to meet others' demands.

The most painful part of this work for most clients is the realization that they have invested so much in others' approval that they have lost the ability to hear their own inner voice. Rage erupts from the fear that there is no self left to hear. This, of course, is never the case. In doing this exercise, Mindy realized that by acknowledging her authentic power she had finally loosened the psychic stranglehold of the limited belief that she could "never do enough." This is tough work. Just like any other life force, the energy behind a powerful limiting belief will fight for its life.

The inspiration for this exercise comes from one of the most powerful life lessons I have internalized: that our greatest vulnerabilities are the flip side of our greatest strengths. This lesson hit home for me one evening during my years as a portfolio manager in Boston when it seemed like the storm clouds of doubt were forming on every horizon of my inner world. On the professional front, Europe was in the midst of a currency crisis, and fund managers around the world were on the verge of hysteria about what might happen if the European Exchange Rate Mechanism came unglued.

As if the international currency markets being in turmoil wasn't enough, I'd just been dumped by my latest boyfriend. There I was, sitting on my sofa in the dark and stubbing out another cigarette in an

The wicked are always surprised to find that the good can be clever.

— Luc de Clapiers de Vauvenargues

empty Lean Cuisine carton. There was an old movie on the television — but I had the sound turned down. I didn't want the noise, but the moving pictures kept me from feeling so alone. Gradually, I realized that I was emotionally numb. My portfolio was down — but the usual rush of adrenaline that had my mind racing through investment scenarios all night just wasn't there. What was even more surprising was that, in that moment, I didn't even care about my love life. The anxiety I usually felt over trying to find my "soulmate" (whatever the hell *that* was!) had given way to a resigned exhaustion that I had somehow ended up acting out the same old tired drama that always left my social life feeling more like work than my job did.

Suddenly, it was as if an inner light had come on and illuminated the darkness all around me from the inside out. I was flooded with such a surge of compassion for myself that I simply started to sob in the dark. The more I cried, the more I realized that I had to give myself credit for something really important — I had survived my own ability to get so focused on my work that I had neglected everything, from my need to sleep and eat to my need for love. I had survived the terrifying anxiety that if anyone knew how emotionally vulnerable I felt at times, they would manipulate me and eventually abandon me. As I sat there in the dark, I realized that I had survived what I had done to myself. I knew my own fears and insecurities better than anyone else possibly could — and over the years I had spent many of my conscious hours torturing myself with them.

As I sat there, I began contemplating who the "me" was that was suddenly conscious of how I had been playing self-defeating games in my relationships over the years. In retrospect, I believe that this moment of grace was my authentic self reaching out to my consciousness at a moment when I was so thoroughly exhausted by the games I was playing that for once I was still enough to listen to myself.

That night was a turning point in my life. In some subtle but powerful way, the "me" that showed up in my consciousness that night stayed. Not only was that "me" able to give me some compassion for

Self-respect is the root of discipline. The sense of dignity grows with the ability to say no to oneself.

—Abraham Joshua Heschel

myself and my vulnerabilities, but it also gave me the strength to make some important changes in my life. For starters, I made a resolution that night to follow my intuition professionally, no matter what. That led to a renewed commitment to make sure that the way my portfolios were positioned was the most accurate reflection of what I thought was going to happen in the market. Not what some other, smarter, person thought — what I thought. This involved some rebalancing of the portfolio, because I realized that I had been seduced into holding several important investment positions because I was anxious to please my boss or to gain political favor with some of the prominent research analysts in our company. Short-term, this cost me politically. Long-term, our group won two Lipper Awards for having the best performing fund in its class nationwide.

One's real life is often the life that one does not lead.

— Oscar Wilde

When I developed the internal courage to admit to myself how terrified I was, I dealt with my role of being a people pleaser by forcing myself to take at least an hour a day when I would get away from the chatter of the trading floor, stop listening to the latest hot research analyst, and ask myself what I really thought. This was scary at first because, after all, in a world full of brilliant strategists, who the hell cares what a frightened little girl from Fort Worth, Texas, thinks? Over the years, I cultivated the discipline of thinking for myself — a discipline that's honed by spotting when your role is kicking in.

Once my team started beating the market, it seemed like everyone cared what I thought. This was more than a little amusing to me. I felt incredibly validated at one point when I found myself speaking on a panel with an equity investor whom I had always admired. He told me privately that he was constantly terrified about getting it wrong. "If you're not scared in this business," he assured me, smiling, "then you've lost your edge."

The good news is that, as tough as the Cueing the Role exercise is, most people who approach it with sincerity only have to do it once. This is because once you start to become aware of your authentic self, you will never allow yourself to become enslaved to the lie of your own unworthiness again.

The even better news for you is that once you've done this exercise you move on to one of the most joyous chapters in this book. The painful part of releasing the roles that no longer serve you is that these aspects of the self must die to make room for new possibilities in your life. The great news is that what you are making room for is your true self. The next chapter will help reawaken and nurture those aspects of your authentic self that have been dormant while your role has been running the show.

It has been my experience that folks who have no vices have very few virtues.

— **Abraham Lincoln**

CHAPTER 6

Strengthening
Your Authentic
Self

By this point in the Authentic Career Process, you have begun to grasp the difference between playing an overly rigid role and enjoying the wider range of options available to your authentic self. However, at this point, being your true self may be the exception rather than the rule. The work in this final chapter of the Emotional Ownership stage is designed to help you strengthen your relationship with your authentic self so that you are able to operate from a more liberating perspective of reality more consistently.

The work in this chapter will help you tap in to your core values and the power of your imagination by reconnecting with your natural myth-making abilities. Our appreciation of the importance of myth, symbols, and our mystical nature is an aspect of our authentic selves that may become frozen in childhood. Far from being childish, these abilities are tools that you can use to create a professional future that reflects your deepest beliefs.

Basically, a myth is the traditional link between the human and the divine. Therefore, it makes sense that understanding myths and how we respond to them can help us understand the link between the roles we play in the world and our authentic selves. Myths are also our way of immortalizing the lives of heroes. My clients have been more and more interested in heroes since the World Trade Center attacks, because many of them who escaped the twin towers witnessed superhuman acts of bravery that are forever imprinted on their memories.

What is a hero? A hero is someone who has transcended the focus on personal gain, so rampant in a competitive society, to devote his or her life to something greater than the self. A hero is someone who has broken free from the chains of selfish thinking so that he or she can reach out to others and save ideas, ideals, and even lives. A hero has the courage to listen to his or her internal wisdom and live authentically.

One of my personal heroes is the popular journalist Bill Moyers, whose brilliant public television documentary *Joseph Campbell and the Power of Myth* inspired this exercise and has enriched my own appreciation of the role of myths in countless ways. In an interview with Moyers, Campbell says, "I have high praise for those men and women who, throughout history, have acted on conscience against the odds."

Moyers noted that Campbell defines a hero as an individual who "does the best of things in the worst of times." History has given us countless examples of periods when it was tough to be heroic — yet heroes emerged anyway. The Spanish Inquisition and the Holocaust, both dark periods in the world's history, were also times when individuals managed to hold on to their humanity and fight for decency, playing an incalculable role in preserving the best aspects of what we like to consider the civilized world today. We can only imagine how difficult it was for these people to muster the courage it took to make a stand for human decency during such terrifying times. However, as with many things, decency counts more under pressure.

Today, many of our struggles are subtler — which makes them all the more daunting. Clearly, the events of September 11th made all of us grateful for the firefighters and rescue workers who performed so heroically on that fateful day. What made this event all the more tragic was that, in losing so many heroes, we became acutely aware of how rarely we see or hear about heroic acts.

Myths are the stories of our leaders — the legends of those who came before us. They form an integral part of the cultural consciousness that shapes us all. These stories not only inspire us, they connect us as a culture. Myths give us a mental framework to focus on as we use the power of group energy to turn our dreams into reality. Myths give us a collective sense of purpose, and, in our darkest times, they give us hope.

But what has happened to our sense of purpose in a world in which so many of our workplaces have become giant bureaucracies where senior management turns over so fast that the organization loses its humanity? Our jobs are the source of financial security and

Security is mostly a superstition. It does not exist in nature, nor do the children of men as a whole experience it. Avoiding danger is no safer in the long run than outright exposure. Life is either a daring adventure or nothing.

— **Helen Keller**

professional identity for many of us, so what happens when our sense of self is defined by an organization that sees us more as parts of a machine than as members of a community? Well, what happens is that we must embrace the reality that we are all self-employed when it comes to defining our sense of purpose and nurturing the sacred in our lives.

Large corporations can offer many advantages in life — and there are many heroes today working within them. If you are an ambitious computer programmer, working in a large corporation can give you the resources to experiment with systems designs you might not be able to explore elsewhere. If you are a portfolio manager, working in a firm with sufficient assets under management may be what you need in order to practice your craft under the most ideal conditions. If you are a filmmaker, you may need to work with a major studio to get your creations financed. However, as you grow in appreciation of your authentic self, you begin to understand that you must give to life as well as take from it. It's important to be realistic about what today's corporate cultures can give to you — and what they desperately need for you to give to them.

Technology, capital, and a great public relations campaign can do many things for us, but these gifts are not enough in and of themselves to help us embrace the mystery of life — or the mystery of what it is to be alive. We all embrace both the practical and the mystical in our lives. However, when we allow the incessant demands of everyday life to lead us away from our commitment to our inner lives, we denigrate the mystical in favor of the practical every time. When we do this long enough, our energy becomes fragmented and we are left intuitively autistic.

The more you cultivate your connection with your authentic self, the more you come to know that you are more than you think you are. Remember that the ideal self is connected to the primal part of your being — and to the forces of nature. Heroic impulses are encoded in our cellular memories as well as in legends. When you create a personal myth, you are using an ancient skill to focus your power, strengthen

Whenever you see a successful business, someone once made a courageous decision.

— Peter Drucker

your courage, and clarify your awareness. Creating myths is something children do naturally. In working with myths, as in so many areas of life, we have much to learn from children.

The shaman, unafraid, experiences death in order to gain control over the elements and the world of the untamed.

— **Joan Halifax**

EXERCISE:

CREATING YOUR PERSONAL MYTH

This exercise is designed to get you reacquainted with the natural myth-making ability you had as a child. In Creating Your Personal Myth, you will be selecting and creating symbols to explain the nature of reality as you understand it. You will also be using these symbols to explain your position within that reality and what you see as your life purpose.

As background for this exercise, you may want to review any myths and legends that resonate with you. Focus on the main characters in these tales; the list is endless and anything goes as long as it is meaningful to you. My clients have been inspired by Adam and Eve, Ulysses, King Arthur, Joan of Arc, Amelia Earhart, Wonder Woman, Luke Skywalker, and even Harry Potter! (Hey, take it from your kids; they are myth-making naturals.) When I do this exercise with groups, we usually watch sections of the Bill Moyers special on Joseph Campbell. Doing this is extremely helpful in understanding more fully the role that myths play in our lives. (You can purchase the video online or from most major booksellers.)

In the middle way of our lives, I found myself in a dark, dangerous wood.

— **Dante**

As you reflect on the myths of your choice, answer the following questions:

1. What conflicts did these characters have?
2. What were their main internal struggles?
3. What obstacles did they face externally?
4. What special talents did these characters have to draw from?
5. What friends and supporters did these characters turn to for help in achieving their goals? How did they interact with and accept the help of others?

6. What opponents did these characters face? How did they interact with them?

7. What was the final fate of these characters? How did their fate
affect others?

It's now time to make you the center of your own myth. Think of
a time when you faced a major challenge. As you recall this event,
reflect on the mythical qualities you displayed and answer as many of
the above questions as seem appropriate to the story featuring you
as the central character. When you have compared your story to a traditional myth, answer the following additional questions:

1. Why did this event happen to me?
2. What forces were at work in other aspects of my life that might
have triggered this event?
3. What aspect of my inner reality did this event clarify for me?
4. What aspect of my outer reality did this event clarify for me?
5. From a mythical perspective, how did this event shape my sense
of self and the lives of those around me?

Finally, you may want to take your answers to these questions and
create your own personal myth or short story from them. Some clients
have found it helpful to do this work in a group. Some people have
told me that they did this in a group of trusted friends and they all
shared their stories with each other. One client even did this exercise
with his family. They had "myth night," in which he, his wife, and
their kids shared their stories with each other.

Be playful with this exercise, and choose symbols that are evocative
for you. One client turned a conflict with his board of directors into a
struggle among the gods on Mount Olympus! (Who said they weren't
the masters of the universe?) Another client made her myth into a personal fairy tale — complete with a set of original illustrations.

John was a member of one of my coaching groups for clients who had
lost their jobs and were in career transition because of mass layoffs at

his company. John found that this exercise gave him some valuable perspective on the ideals that were shaping his professional behavior.

JOHN

"I had dinner with a couple of the other guys in the group after you gave us this exercise at the end of our session," John told me. "We all agreed that we'd done some pretty creative stuff working with you, but most of us were skeptical about doing a short story. I guess what got to me was when you mentioned what naturals kids are at myths. I know I've been spending much more time with my kids since I left my job, and their ability to use stories to keep them going has been an ongoing source of inspiration for me."

"Did you get your kids to help you with this one?" I asked him, smiling.

"Yeah, I actually did my first series of questions with my son's help," John told me, grinning. "You said to keep it playful, and no one can keep it more playful than he can. I was glad that the Bill Moyers video we watched had Joseph Campbell mentioning *Star Wars* as a good example of a myth. I've always loved the *Star Wars* movies, and I got a real thrill taking my son to the new one last year. It took me back to the thrill I got as a kid when the first one came out.

"My son, Andy, and I watched the video of the original *Star Wars* movie together over the weekend, and then we talked about the conflicts and challenges that the main characters were facing. Andy had just turned ten. I was amazed at how insightful he was about what was going on in that movie. It was remarkable to hear him say, 'It must have been hard for Luke Skywalker to believe he could do all that amazing stuff. After all, he'd spent most of his life in a place where nobody believed in special powers at all.' You know, I don't think I was that thoughtful about the plot of the first *Star Wars* when I was a kid."

One man with courage makes a majority.

— attributed to Andrew Jackson

The fire of wisdom burns all imperfections to ashes.

— Unknown

"How did this exercise help you put your situation at the office into perspective?" I asked him.

"After Andy and I had done our part together, I took some time on my own to reflect on a challenge at work that I found worthy of mythologizing," John told me. "I decided to write about how I'd managed to get ahead in spite of the fact that I didn't have an Ivy League degree. This was something I'd felt self-conscious about for years, and I was really proud of the fact that I'd made enough money to support my family in style in spite of that.

"When I considered this challenge from a mythical perspective, I realized that there were some factions of people on Wall Street that operated from hard work and hustle, and others that operated, at least in my perspective, from the snobby assumption that they were smarter than everyone else because of their degree or their social circle. One thing that has always burned me is when somebody in senior management promotes a kid based on family connections when there are other hard-working people who deserve the recognition more. I've seen that happen more than once in my career. I'd always felt a special surge of victory on the trading floor when I'd outsmarted some guy who came from a wealthy family and, in the process, helped another hard-working person get the credit they deserved based on their street smarts — not on their pedigree.

"When it got to writing my own myth, I made myself into Robin Hood! I'd managed to use my own innate street smarts to make enough money to help out my family and lots of guys in my neighborhood. When I was able to do this by outsmarting guys that I thought were greedy and unethical, it felt like taking from the rich and giving to the poor!"

"Were you surprised by the reaction you got when you shared this story with the other men in the group?" I asked. The validation that clients get from seeing other people react to their stories is frequently one of the most valuable parts of this exercise.

"We were all surprised at how much we enjoyed the session when we read our myths to each other," John told me. "I'd actually had a blast with mine, but I wasn't sure how some of the other guys were going to respond. It was amazing to hear a group of macho guys reading these amazingly philosophical and sensitive stories they'd written. It was also fascinating how easy it was to pinpoint the actual workplace situations behind the myths that everyone had written. Of course, as soon as our session was over, a bunch of us went out to grab some beers and make fun of each other like crazy — but we were all moved by how close we felt to each other by doing this."

Many of the exercises in this book can be done individually or in groups — and this one is no exception. You will get a great deal out of this one if you do it on your own. If you don't have a group to share it with, perhaps you can share your work with someone you feel comfortable with from your peer group.

The example I used for this exercise comes from one of my group sessions because myths are essentially about how we share information about the nature of reality in a community. The use of symbols in myth is a powerful way to focus the energy of the authentic self, and sharing our work with others is a powerful way to use group energy to amplify our convictions.

John's comment about how easy it was to figure out which life events had inspired the myths the guys in his group created is important. Our feelings are one of the most vital aspects of our humanity. Feelings shape the invisible plane of reality and breathe life into the concrete structures that surround us. Myths connect us to our feelings at a primal level. We need this connection in the modern world — particularly if we are consummate performers who have learned the art of sharing our experiences as dispassionately as possible in order to appear professional.

When we share our myths with others, we are participating in a ritual that reinforces our commitment to our truth at the cellular level.

As a culture we tend to be strongly outer-directed; we are not trained to venture inward to find the next steps of our growth. As a result, much truth lies hidden within us, in the depths of our self. Of that unknown, hidden self, there is much that must be unfolded in order for us to embody the truth.

— **Charles Bates**

*Unfortunately our
Western mind,
lacking all culture in this
respect, has never yet
devised a concept,
nor even a name,
for the "union of opposites
through the middle path,"
that most fundamental item
of inward experience,
which could respectably be
set against the Chinese
concept of the Tao.*

— Carl Jung

Our personal power is fed by the attention and support we receive from the people who are listening to us. We can get many valuable things from the information available to us on the Internet and in books — but we cannot get the energetic boost we derive from interacting with other human beings. This interaction is vital to nurturing our personal power.

Without this type of ritualistic exchange of energy, many of us feel starved. Many coaches and healers with whom I have worked are concerned that one of the reasons violence is on the rise in our culture, particularly among young people, is that we spend far more time surrounded by machines than we do in meaningful exchange with other human beings. So many of our rituals have lost the power of the present moment. That's why it's important for us to draw on the wisdom of our authentic selves to create new rituals — and to share the power we gain from these experiences with others.

Your work in the Emotional Ownership Stage has helped you to identify previously suppressed feelings. Learning to access the full range of your emotions is vital to authentic success, because when we suppress important feelings, we cut off our access to our creativity and inner wisdom in the process. Learning to identify your feelings also builds the emotional courage necessary to remain true to your authentic self when dealing with others. This emotional courage is a prerequisite for proceeding successfully to the work in the Interaction Stage.

STAGE III
INTERACTION

At the heart of the Interaction Stage are two mutually reinforcing goals. The first is learning to operate from your authentic self as you interact with others. Getting in touch with your true self will do little to further you personally or professionally unless you are able to maintain this perspective while you deal with the conflicts, challenges, and competition that take place in typical workplace situations.

The second goal is to understand how the dominant beliefs in your workplace environment affect your sense of self. Your work in the first half of the Authentic Career Process has showed how your self-image has been shaped by the core beliefs and emotional boundaries that you internalized from your family. In the Interaction Stage, you will learn how your work culture has similarly influenced you to play a role that is acceptable to a group — particularly when that group is under pressure.

An intimate relationship is one in which neither party silences, sacrifices or betrays the self.

— Harriet Lerner

Over time, the values, pace, and perspective of your work environment will subtly seep into your psyche. If you work in a fast-paced, stressful environment, you may find that your mind is racing even in your private moments. Many people in challenging jobs report that they have difficulty being present to their family and loved ones outside the office. Similarly, if you are moving ahead in your job and feel appreciated professionally, this will enhance the self-confidence that you bring to everything from an encounter with your mother-in-law to a blind date.

The work in the Interaction Stage is based on a fundamental assumption: *group energy* powerfully shapes your sense of self and plays a vital role in all interpersonal dynamics. By using the term *group energy,* I am referring to the dominant beliefs, values, and emotional tone that characterize any group, from your family members to your co-workers.

Your workplace, where you spend some of the most valuable hours of your life, is alive with its own brand of group energy. Understanding the role that group energy plays either in amplifying or in undermining your success gives you a whole new perspective on work cultures. Once you understand the powerful impact group energy can have on your self-esteem, your perspective of reality, and even the emotional tone of your personal relationships, you can begin evaluating the merits of various types of careers in a refreshingly different way. Clarifying the way group energy shapes your sense of self also protects you from being inducted into another person's view of reality and losing touch with your own priorities in the process.

The Interaction Stage will help you learn to deal with others whose objectives conflict with yours without compromising your values in the process. This work also lays the foundation of personal integrity necessary to proceed successfully to the next stage, Integration. The Interaction Stage is divided into three chapters:

- *Chapter 7: "Understanding the Impact of Group Energy."* The first goal of the Interaction Stage is to help you understand the way your perspective of reality either has resonated or clashed with the dominant values in your organizational system. The exercises in the first chapter are designed to help you identify the acceptable range of emotional expression in your workplace and how your success has been enhanced or stymied by participating in this environment.

- *Chapter 8: "Building Relationships That Support Your Authentic Self."* Once you have become more aware of how powerfully group energy influences your perspective of reality and your sense of self, you will have a deeper understanding of the importance both of peer support and of feedback. The second goal of the Interaction Stage is to help you cultivate and nurture personal and professional relationships that will further your life goals.

- *Chapter 9: "Remaining True to Yourself Under Pressure."* The final goal of this stage is to help you build your understanding of the

It is well to remember that the entire population of the universe, with one trifling exception, is composed of others.

— Andrew J. Holmes

You can live a lifetime and, at the end of it, know more about other people than you know of yourself.

— Beryl Markham

role that energy plays in interpersonal challenges. Group energy creates powerful waves both of support and sabotage. However, it's important to remember that the first place energy is shifted is within the self. An understanding of how energy influences the professional impression you are making on others will help you maintain important relationships without sacrificing your personal power in the process.

Just as you as an individual play various roles to suppress uncomfortable feelings, your organization creates roles at the group level that powerfully influence the emotional expression and viewpoints deemed acceptable.

The personality of any organization is merely a reflection of the thinking of its leaders. Sadly, as organizational leaders play musical chairs faster and faster in our economy, their ability to bring their humanity as well as their logical problem-solving skills to bear on the organizations they work within is dwindling. In the last five years, we have seen increasing turnover in CEOs and senior management. While management changes can be invigorating, they can also be disruptive. Just as you're never going to fully appreciate the mystery of marriage if you can't commit to your partner, a leader is never going to leave the mark of his or her humanity on an organization by starting the job focused solely on his or her exit strategy.

The only thing that will preserve the soul of a company is for its leaders to bring their humanity to bear in their daily management. Nearly every leader today has taken a very personal route involving a unique combination of vision, determination, and luck.

It is vital to your professional success that you understand the psychic landscape of the group you work with as you attempt to advance your career. You need to develop a keen awareness of your firm's role, because it will influence both your timing and your tactics as you take strategic action to further your success. You will also need to understand the way your company's role differs from the authentic mission that your company is, theoretically at least, in business to pursue. To stand out authentically you need to see from the perspective of your authentic self and focus on your organization's genuine mission. However, for your best ideas ever to be acknowledged, you must be able to

CHAPTER 7

Understanding the Impact of Group Energy

communicate these ideas effectively within the complex web of emotional alliances that form your workplace culture. This web is what I sometimes refer to as an organization's "meta-role." Remember how the work you did in the Awareness Stage was a prerequisite for getting below the neck in your relationship with yourself? Similarly, the work we are doing in the Interaction Stage helps you to make a greater impact on your organization by enabling you to work with its unofficial currents of influence and information.

EXERCISE:

DEFINING THE ORGANIZATIONAL ROLE

Think about the answers to these questions from the perspective of your authentic self as much as possible, because doing so will give you maximum insight into both the limits and the potential of your work environment.

The trouble with the rat race is that even if you win, you're still a rat.

— Lily Tomlin

You may want to take your journal to work if you have a quiet place where you can work on this exercise during the day, since it can be helpful to be submerged in the group energy of your workplace as you answer these questions. Since most of my clients are convinced that the work in this exercise benefits their organizations as much as it benefits them, doing this exercise on the job rarely presents a moral dilemma.

Answer the following questions:

YOUR WORKPLACE ENVIRONMENT

1. How would you describe the emotional tone of your organization your first day on the job? How does it differ from the way you would characterize your company's emotional tone today?

2. Describe the physical setting of your workplace. What does it convey about the values of your organization?

3. What is the emotional tone of the anecdotes that pass through your office grapevine?

4. Is the dominant group energy you function within dictated by your immediate supervisor, your department, or by the overall office environment?

5. How are conflicts negotiated in your workplace? What personal characteristics and interpersonal skills do the people who tend to win the "turf wars" display?

6. What are the dominant subcultures in your organization, and how do they influence the informal power structure and the flow of communication day-to-day?

7. What is the formal career track in your organization, and what is the informal route to power? How do these differ?

8. Who has the power to challenge rules and acknowledge problems in your workplace?

*Colleges hate geniuses,
just as convents hate saints.*

— Ralph Waldo Emerson

SENIOR MANAGEMENT

1. What are the official values of senior management? What unofficial values do the leaders in your organization share? How do these values influence the kind of people that succeed in your organization?

2. What personality characteristics would define a "rising star" in your workplace? How do these characteristics reflect the dominant values of senior management?

3. How are senior management's values communicated throughout the organization? How much consistency or inconsistency is there in how these values are communicated?

4. Who sets the performance standards in your organization, and who evaluates them? Does the performance review process increase intimacy or foster distance between managers and employees?

YOUR ORGANIZATION RELATIVE TO THE INDUSTRY

1. How does your company perform relative to its competitors?
2. What are the weaknesses of your workplace culture? How do these relate to the culture's strengths?
3. How does the mix of strengths and weaknesses in your company compare with that of your firm's main competitors in its industry?
4. What attracted you to this job? As an insider, how does your sense of this work environment compare to your sense of it before you started working there?

It is vital to remain in touch with your instincts and to be as objective as possible when answering these questions. The value of answering these questions is an increased "below-the-neck," or emotional, perspective. Remember that the central goal here is to understand the origin of the group energy that affects you professionally and to learn how to respond to it most productively.

Amy is a fund-raiser in a nonprofit organization. She came for coaching when her organization began downsizing. After weeks of wondering whether she was going to be part of the next round of layoffs, she was relieved to find that she was going to be given a new team to run, which would involve building a whole new set of alliances. Amy found the Defining the Organizational Role exercise particularly helpful, because even though she was working for the same firm, she felt like she was starting over in a completely new culture.

AMY

"I was fairly startled by the realities that hit me as I did this exercise," Amy told me. "Because it's a nonprofit, you would think that the group energy of our workplace environment would be nurturing and people focused. Nothing could be further from the truth. As fund-raising has

In a real sense all life is inter-related. All men are caught in an inescapable network of mutuality, tied in a single garment of destiny. Whatever affects one directly affects all indirectly. I can never be what I ought to be until you are what you ought to be, and you can never be what you ought to be until I am what I ought to be. This is the inter-related structure of reality.

— **Martin Luther King, Jr.**

become tougher, our nonprofit has begun to feel as competitive as any Fortune 500 firm.

"The only two people in my organization I could think of who could tell me anything about the origins of the firm were clerical research staff in our library. Both of these women are dedicated academics who have been collating information for our CEO and fund-raising group for almost six years now. Despite the fact that they know more about the important players in philanthropy than most people in the industry, they are both viewed and compensated as support staff. The other week, we hired an aggressive young guy from the private sector to spearhead a project that involves working with a small fraction of the information that these women know by heart. This guy is being paid much more than the rest of our team to take a more aggressive approach to our fund-raising strategy.

"Officially, senior management talks nonstop about teamwork. In reality, the people who get ahead are consummate politicians who are brilliant at getting other people to do their work for them. To make it to a senior position at our firm, someone else has to do most of your work, or you'd never have time for all of the internal schmoozing it takes to get promoted.

"My first day working with this new hire from the private sector was downright frightening. While he was hired to be my peer, from day one he was really aggressive about trying to position himself as my boss. That aggressive tone tends to characterize most of the 'rising stars' in this place. It's not that the people who get ahead here aren't nice — many of them are — but you almost need to have razor blades on your elbows to deal with the jostling for position that takes place over every little thing. My superiors know this, and I think they like it. Our chairman was actually quoted as saying, 'You can't be too aggressive at this business.' The grapevine buzzes with that statement every day. I bet he has no idea that this one simple statement is quoted like a mantra.

"This attitude has also contributed to a 'what have you done for me lately?' attitude with some of our long-time donors who have had

You can discover what your enemy fears most by observing the means he uses to frighten you.

— Eric Hoffer

to cut back on their contributions because of setbacks in the business environment. I've been mortified when I have had to tell people who have made significant contributions in the past to the organizations we support that I can't include them in an upcoming event because they haven't given us enough money this year. It seems ungrateful and unprofessional.

"An incident last week perfectly summed up the attitude in our office. A group of private citizens had banded together to do a fund-raiser for one of the groups we support. While the amount of money they raised was modest, the amount of effort they put in to the fund-raising event was touching. They had an awards ceremony and wanted to present the check to our CEO. He waved me off impatiently when I told him he needed to clear his calendar to be present at this cere-mony. I had to accept the check without him, and I did my best to thank this group for their efforts. When I got back to the office with the check, rather than asking me how the event had gone, he simply grunted, took the check from me, and threw it in his desk drawer. At that moment, I knew there was a serious schism between what we were trying to do as a fund-raising organization and the spirit with which we were doing it.

"I went into nonprofit work because it's important for me to feel that I am making a difference for the people in our community. How-ever, doing this exercise made me realize that making a difference isn't just about the amount of money we raise; it's about how we go about doing it. I realize that the ruthless attitude that has started to infect our company is being driven by the fear we all feel in a tough economic environment. However, I also realize that as I get stronger in my con-nection with my authentic self, I'm determined to rise to a position of authority where I can make sure that our firm recognizes and rewards human values as well as financial ones. This is not going to be easy, but I am determined to make this a personal mission. I went into this line of work to make a difference. Now I'm beginning to realize that part of making a difference involves helping my colleagues realize that, in this line of work, doing their work with heart is part of their

Every man becomes, to a certain degree, what the people he generally converses with are.

— Lord Philip Dormer Stanhope of Chesterfield

professional responsibility. Of course, doing this work helped me realize that I have to continue strengthening my commitment to philanthropy to help heal the culture of my firm."

Some work environments are tough. It's easy to be a critic. Therefore, it's just as important to try being nonjudgmental and gentle in assessing your organization's meta-role as it is to come to terms with the role you may have played to get ahead. The harsh aspects of any of the roles people fall into, either individually or collectively, are rarely a reflection of any innate mean-spiritedness. Remember, any job environment we encounter is the creation of our collective consciousness — even if that consciousness is creating something rather rigid. Just as you learned from your work with shifting your individual role, you can't foster effective change by pointing fingers and blaming. Rather, you do it by accepting the logical reason for the way things are and then finding a more effective way of addressing your organization's authentic purpose.

As we grow, we also begin to understand that it is when we are playing our rather limited individual roles that we judge workplace cultures and the individuals who are part of them most harshly. In my own professional transition, I developed powerful professional friendships with people I had competed fiercely against for business earlier. I can remember having lunch with a fellow survivor of a corporate turf war in the early 1990s who told me, "You know, we thought we were political then. However, when I look back on the situation, we were too focused on the job and too naive to really play hardball with each other. Today, I'm fighting with professional politicians in the boardroom. It's a whole different level of competition."

Many of the most outstanding (and enlightened) executives I have worked with have learned the powerful lesson that the people who were their enemies in a corporate turf war one year may be their greatest supporters the following year. What's more, I'm often reminding

I have the feeling that we are in such a hurry that we do not even have time to look at one another and smile.

— Mother Teresa

my clients to embrace the aggressive behavior they experience in the workplace as an opportunity to shine as someone who diffuses tense situations with humor and professionalism. Remember, professionalism counts most under pressure. When things are going smoothly, you don't have an opportunity to stand out in your ability to deal with stress.

One of the benefits of being in touch with your authentic instincts is that it gives you the personal power you need to accept your shortcomings as well as your strengths with grace. Learning to forgive yourself is a prerequisite for being able to cut your colleagues some slack. The critical tone or harsh words that you overhear when a colleague berates her peers is usually a faint echo of the inner voice that this individual, in her role, uses in self-critical moments. In fact, the work you have done on your role versus your authentic self has probably taught you that the way you communicate with others simply mirrors important aspects of your relationship with yourself.

Now that you have a clearer picture of the organizational role, it's time to analyze your personal relationships in your department and the overall workplace culture. To describe the passion that fuels authentic success, I remind my clients that not only does the group energy of your organization have a powerfully formative influence on you, but your energy also contributes to your department and your firm in a myriad of ways.

If you realize what the problem is — losing yourself, giving yourself to some higher end, or to another — you realize that this itself is the ultimate trial. When we quit thinking primarily about ourselves and our own self-preservation, we undergo a truly heroic transformation of consciousness.

— Joseph Campbell

Because of this powerful two-way influence, it is vital for you to understand that there is no way to be in any meaningful relationship without sacrificing some of your individuality. Let's face it: you can't have a relationship with a romantic partner, a child, or even a family pet without making some accommodations. Thus, the idea that you would be able to function as a member of a competitive organization without making some individual sacrifices is ludicrous.

The trick to maximizing your success and your satisfaction simultaneously is in understanding where and when to accommodate the group without losing the spark of individuality that makes you a positive and creative addition to your team. To find this "sweet spot," you must know your organization — and yourself. The next exercise, the

Influence Chart, gives you a chance to build on the reflective work you've done on your roles and your interpersonal relationships on the job to see where strategic improvements can increase your success.

EXERCISE:

THE INFLUENCE CHART

Before starting this exercise, first review the work you did in the Personal Tree of Life exercise in chapter 1. The Influence Chart is similar to a regular organizational chart showing the official hierarchical relationships in your department. However, an Influence Chart is meant to map the way your department functions as a social system rather than as a business unit. For instance, on a traditional organizational chart, a new vice president would rank higher than an administrative assistant. On the Influence Chart, however, if the vice president is not yet one of the inner circle, and the administrative assistant has personal sway with the senior management team, this ranking might be reversed.

To construct an Influence Chart for your department, start with the official organizational chart — but then score each member of the department on a scale of 1 to 3, based on the amount of daily interpersonal influence he or she exerts. A 3 means that this individual is a valued and powerful member of the department's social system, while a 1 indicates that this person is an outsider — possibly even a departmental scapegoat.

Now take your journal and list all the 3's in a row across the top of the page. Follow this by listing all the 2's across the middle, and the 1's in a row along the bottom of the page. Then take a minute to answer the following questions:

1. Where do you fall on the Influence Chart, and why?
2. What core beliefs and patterns of interaction noted on your Personal Tree of Life may be contributing to your position in your department's social hierarchy?
3. What role do you play in your department's social system? How

A great-souled hero must transcend the slavish thinking of those around him.

— Friedrich Nietzsche

is this similar to or different from the role you play in your family system?

4. Can you identify any shared personality characteristics among the most influential people in your department?

5. What relational patterns can you work with to improve your position on the Influence Chart?

Most people complete this exercise in a few days. However, be careful not to rush yourself in making assessments about why you consider certain people powerful within your organization.

When Stanley compared his Personal Tree of Life with the Influence Chart that he constructed following a few departmental meetings, he noticed several key patterns.

STANLEY

All the people like us are We, and everyone else is They.

— Rudyard Kipling

"One of the reasons that I feel like I can't trust my boss is that I haven't been able to trust anyone in a position of authority since my father died," Stanley admitted in our individual session. "My mother emotionally abandoned me after my father passed away, and it felt like it was just me against the world after that. I guess that other people can sense that I have trouble trusting them, particularly my boss. That's probably why it's tough for him to give me the benefit of the doubt.

"I worked weekly with updates on my Influence Chart. Sometimes it felt like I was being a little obsessive, but it actually helped me to Xerox a blank chart that I filled in every week to track the popularity 'horse race' in my department. This gave me a system for tracking ways to improve my relationships with people at all levels of my department, from my subordinates to my boss.

"One of the first things this strategy helped me to notice is that the most influential people in our department spent more informal time with the boss than I did. I used to consider this 'sucking up,' and I felt it was beneath me. This work helped me be more objective about my emotional reluctance to being more political. When I began to look at interacting with my boss more strategically and less emotionally, I realized that one of the reasons I had been so emotional about this in the past was that, ever since my father died, I had really longed for a relationship with a male authority figure. Because this was so important to me emotionally, I avoided my boss because I had been secretly terrified of being rejected by a male authority figure. Once I realized what was really holding me back, I was able to look for opportunities to get 'face time' just like the other people in my department.

"I began my face-time strategy by coming up with topics of conversation to initiate with my boss. I selected topics that were relevant to our department's profitability, would highlight my hard work, and would help me build the kind of mutually respectful rapport with my boss that was necessary if he was going to consider me as a candidate for running our group.

"Using the Influence Chart to track everyone's informal standing in our group also made me aware of the critical importance of timing. I noticed that people who rushed eagerly into our boss's office on a bad day usually regretted this. Because I was tracking this strategically, not emotionally, I began looking for moments when our boss was in a good mood, and trying to approach him then. The payoff of being strategic about my timing was huge.

"Of course, there's more to this than simply manipulating my timing, and sometimes I have to deal with our boss when a crisis is breaking. While the Influence Chart made me mindful of when I was broaching tough topics with my boss, it also made me more mindful of how I was doing it. For example, I began to notice that the people who consistently scored as having the most influence in our department were the ones who did not quake in fear and could be more relaxed when he had one of his angry outbursts in response to the stress we are all under. For example, there is one young guy in the boss's inner

You will become as small as your controlling desire; as great as your dominant aspiration.

— James Allen

circle who is just learning our business, but I've seen him listen to him blow off steam but stay relaxed and sometimes even get him to laugh on a tough day. Needless to say, our boss loves this guy.

"These observations bothered me at first, because I'd always felt that success at work should be about professional performance, not about personal relationships. For example, when some people got larger pay cuts than others last year, we were all told, 'Don't take it personally.' However, as I worked with the Influence Chart, I realized that many business decisions do have a powerful personal component, and that I'm kidding myself if I don't accept that.

"Trying to bear in mind the way people in our group who had the most influence with our boss reacted, I took the risk of taking him aside one afternoon when he blew up at me in front of my team. Frankly, my team likes me, and when he does this we lose hours and occasionally even days of productivity while they all gossip about his latest mood swings instead of doing their work. Based on the way I'd seen our boss react with his inner circle, the day after his outburst I told him, 'I'm glad that you feel comfortable enough to let off steam in front of me. I understand how much pressure you are under, and how committed we all are to making a profit in a tough market. However, when you need to unload, do it with me in private. I know where you are coming from, and I can take it. Let me pass your comments on to our team in my own way.' I also made sure that I said this in a relaxed, easygoing manner and that I kept my comments brief."

Doing the Influence Chart gives many people some powerful insights into dealing with volatile situations with their superiors. By watching the behavior of people who seem to exert a positive influence on your supervisors, you are often better able to deal with the mood swings of powerful people under pressure with enough compassion to keep these influential (and often sensitive) individuals from feeling personally attacked.

"My relationship with my boss has steadily improved since I started acting less anxious around him. At first this felt kind of false. Since his temper really does scare me, I felt that acting less afraid was insincere. I also wanted to be true to myself and not slip into a role of acting macho when I was really feeling emotionally assaulted."

"What's the key difference between playing a role that isn't genuine and being your authentic self in this case?" I asked him. This question is one of the most important for clients to come to terms with as they build on the work they did in the Emotional Ownership Stage by doing these exercises.

"What it came down to for me was being conscious of what I was doing and why I was doing it and remaining honest with myself about this. This made me realize that it was when I was playing my role that I automatically reacted fearfully to my boss before I realized what I was doing, and that when I was making a conscious decision to respond in a less anxious manner, I was being more authentic. I've made a note to myself on my computer now that reads, 'If I'm out of control, it must be my role,'" he told me, grinning.

"I also realized that my boss's outbursts, and many people's anxiety, had gotten much more amplified as the overall atmosphere in our office had become more stressful. Combining this insight with what I learned from observing the behavior of his inner circle by making an Influence Chart has helped me be more relaxed under pressure and reinforced my commitment to adhering to my true values.

"This work is also saving my company a fortune. My boss may not realize it yet, but I've been much more effective at keeping my team focused on their work and less focused on the chatter that distracts them when they are all wondering whether or not the boss is going to blow today. In the long run, this should contribute to the kind of profitability that will boost both my official and my unofficial influence," he told me, smiling.

One of the reasons our society has become such a mess is that we're isolated from one another.

— **Maggie Kuhn**

One of the most common reasons that people come for coaching is that, while they are competent at meeting the functional requirements of their jobs, they are often blind to the vital importance of gaining the support of their peers. The next step was for Stanley to develop the internal resources he needs to overcome his emotional resistance to being political. As Stanley did this work, he began to understand the difference between slipping into his role and developing the internal resources to react to others more effectively and in a manner that reinforced his commitment to his true values. Developing these internal resources involved building the confidence to define his goals clearly, feeling worthy of achieving these goals, and focusing his internal and external resources on achieving success.

To build this confidence, Stanley had to do what all of us must do to take charge of our careers and our lives. We have to rebuild our ability to trust. Rebuilding trust begins with rebuilding our ability to trust ourselves.

Part of the inspiration behind creating the Influence Chart came from my experience when I switched from being a buy-side money manager to a sell-side marketer dealing with pension fund managers and third-party consultants. After a few glowing meetings with senior executives who had had a positive relationship with me as a fund manager, I was right in the trench with every other hopeful executive pitching institutional clients — I was cold calling. While my knowledge of the business (and, I hoped, my "sparkling personality") tended to help me close business when I got important meetings, getting those meetings in a business environment that was driven as much by personal relationships as it was by performance results was a tough game.

In dealing with third-party consultants, I quickly learned that the entire consulting firm was my client — not just the senior executive who was the gatekeeper to the latest juicy pension fund account. This realization led to a dramatic shift in my skills. For years, my primary talent had been assessing the way that various currencies and interest rates were going to move relative to one another. Now I was focused on the subtle levels of influence and lines of communication that formed the lifeblood of the organizations I needed to develop relationships with to help my firm land business.

People need to learn how to protect their own boundaries from intrusion in terms of both technology and the negative energy that can be created from the waves of mass greed and anxiety that are created by irresponsible messages on our airwaves.

— Evan Imber-Black

Understanding nuances such as which junior analyst was a rising star and had the ear of the CEO and which senior consultant was on his way out and couldn't help our firm land business (even though they could still be a great source of information and referrals) became so integral to my success that I began drawing my own unofficial organizational charts around what I believed to be the true lines of power within these various groups. These private charts sometimes correlated with the levels of seniority on the official organizational chart — and sometimes they did not.

The hardest fight a man has to fight is to live in a world where every single day someone is trying to make you someone you do not want to be.

— e. e. cummings

CHAPTER 8

Building Relationships That Support Your Authentic Self

Once you begin to understand the power that group energy has both in shaping your sense of self and in helping you focus your energy, you start to realize that one of the keys to personal power is strengthening your ability to trust yourself. To strengthen this ability, it's vital to have a strong peer support group.

There's probably no more revealing indicator of how you feel about yourself than the people with whom you choose to surround yourself and the way they mirror back to you who you are and what you stand for. From this perspective, one of the most important investments you make in your life will be the time and energy you spend cultivating friends and professional peers that reinforce your ability to trust yourself. Observing the way that your authentic self reacts to others will help you make wise investments in building relationships that reinforce your self-esteem rather than undermining it.

EXERCISE:
YOUR SUPPORT GROUP INVENTORY

It may take you a few days to gather some of the materials you will need for this exercise, unless your personal mementos are extremely organized! Although you don't need all of the following, it would be extremely helpful (if these items are available and appropriate) for you to assemble any school yearbooks that are meaningful to you and any significant pictures of friends or letters you have received. It would also be helpful to have a couple of conversations with your parents, if they are still living (or the parents who raised you, if you are adopted), about the friendships that were significant to them. Take some brief notes during these conversations in preparation for taking your Support Group Inventory.

Once you've assembled these materials, use the pictures and notes you have gathered to help you answer the following questions:

1. What kind of friends did your parents have, and what were these friendships based on?
2. If you have siblings, what were their friendships like? What did these relationships teach you about friendship?
3. What was one of the most important childhood friendships that you can remember?
4. What were some of the most important friendships you can remember from your school years?
5. Do any friendships from childhood, high school, or college remain important to you today?
6. How has your definition of friendship evolved over time?
7. How many close friends do you have today? List these friends by name.
8. Are your friends generous with their time and the attention they pay to you? Are you generous with your time and the attention you pay to your friends? Explain why or why not.
9. Do you share any values with your friends? If so, what are they? If your values differ from those of your friends, what are these differences?
10. Which friends support your authentic self, and which support the role that you play professionally?
11. Based on your current sense of self, what kind of people do you think would most want to be around you? What do you have to offer these people by being their friend?

What people say behind your back is your standing in the community.

— Edgar Watson Howe

At this point, you need to take a brief break to let your answers to the above questions settle a bit. Have a snack, take a short walk, and then come back to complete this exercise by answering the following:

1. Which friends do I need to acknowledge and make more time for in my life?
2. Which friendships do I need to re-evaluate because they no longer support my authentic self?

3. What kind of qualities am I looking for in someone whom I would consider a friend?
4. What kind of qualities do I need to cultivate in myself in order to be a better friend to others?

If this exercise helps you realize that there are any people in your life who are important to you whom you haven't acknowledged recently, this might be a great time to write a few notes or fire off a couple of emails to them.

Whoever you are — I have always depended on the kindness of strangers.

— Blanche Dubois in
A Streetcar Named Desire,
by Tennessee Williams

Jeff works in the marketing department for a large appliance manufacturing firm. He came for coaching because he believed that his relationship with his immediate boss had become so toxic that it was undermining his position at his firm. Doing this exercise helped Jeff understand that one of the reasons his boss's political games had been so emotionally draining for him was that he had felt personally isolated for some time.

JEFF

"I realized right off the bat that my parents hadn't had many friends and hadn't modeled friendship for me in any way," Jeff began in the session after he completed this exercise. "My father was a highly self-absorbed salesman type, and, after a series of affairs, he eventually left my mother for his secretary when I was about eight years old. My mom was an alcoholic, and she didn't get into recovery until a few years ago. There were so many family secrets around my house that we had people over as little as possible. Basically, Mom's friend was the bottle. It wasn't a great scene.

"As the oldest of three," Jeff continued, "I had made some friends through sports — but I was always nervous about what they'd think of me if they knew how messed up my family was. I just learned not to talk about my personal stuff too much with other people. My friendships were based on finding people to hang out with who didn't ask too many questions about my family and my background. Once you got too personal with me, I was gone!

"By the time I got to college, I was pretty insecure. I was a great athlete, so that made me popular with some people, but I had trouble really getting close to anyone. The few friendships I had were pretty much based on sports. I also had some trouble with my schoolwork — and that made me self-conscious as well. I learned several years ago that I had attention deficit disorder. I wish I'd known that sooner, since it might have changed a lot of things and made it easier for me to reach out to other people.

"I married one of the first girls I dated in college, and before I knew what had hit me, we had four kids and I had tons of responsibilities to juggle. Our marriage wasn't even really based on much of a friendship. I love Stephanie, but I married a woman who is as much into keeping things to herself as I am. She doesn't have much of a circle of friends either. When she gets upset, she sneaks into our garage and smokes. I hate it when she does that, but I can't say that I don't understand.

"My boss, Tom, was one of the few guys I socialized with before he convinced me to work for him. I started working with Tom about eight years ago, and it took me a long time to realize that he was stealing all my best ideas and positioning himself with senior management as if he had thought of them himself. I was utterly enraged by this, but I didn't have anyone to talk it over with, as this kind of thing just sends Stephanie into the garage in a nicotine fit.

"Tom's better at schmoozing senior management than I am, so he eventually got promoted above me. It's been hell at work ever since he has become my boss. I've thought a lot about what I would value in a friend, and Tom's got none of these qualities. Sadly, because I'd had so few friendships, I think that I was fooled when he started sucking up to me years ago to get me to work with him. I'm kind of shy, so I never really got why he wanted to be my friend in the first place. Now I get it loud and clear — he wanted to use me!"

Loneliness and the feeling of being unwanted is the most terrible poverty.

— Mother Teresa

"Who are the friends you turn to for feedback and support outside the office?" I asked him. I frequently ask clients to list their friends to remind them that if all of their dinner dates and personal time away from their families is work related, their perspective on their lives can become dangerously undiversified.

"Doing this exercise has helped me realize that I need a support group of men who I respect so I can bounce career ideas off of someone. I've never had that. The problem is, I still don't know why anyone would want to be friends with me. What's more, Tom's daily digs at my self-esteem aren't helping my confidence any.

"To spend time with people who validate me more, I've decided to touch base with a couple of the guys who played on the basketball team with me in college. Some of them have tried to keep up with me over the years, but when family responsibilities kept growing, I just never made getting back to them a priority. However, this work has helped me realize that, without the support of family and friends, I'm emotionally vulnerable to being exploited by others. If taking the time to build friendships that strengthen my self-esteem is what it takes to help me improve my life and my career, I'm willing to make the effort."

As long as you keep a person down, some part of you has to be down there to hold him down, so it means you can't soar as you otherwise might.

— Marian Anderson

When your sense of self plummets in the face of some personal or professional setback, friends play a crucial role. To compete in our fast-paced culture, where the stakes are high, we must have a support system that helps reinforce our core self-esteem. In many ways, we form our sense of self through the feedback we get from others. If all the feedback we get comes from professional colleagues who have a stake in keeping us insecure, and we don't develop the support systems we need to counteract this, we are putting ourselves in an extremely vulnerable position.

To help you define the characteristics of your authentic self, take some time to review the exercises you have done. As you look over your list of friends, take special note of the ones who genuinely support you. Consider each friend or relative in your support group and ask yourself, "Do I feel stronger and better about myself after I have been in contact with this person, or does contact with him or her leave me feeling unsure, frustrated, or inadequate?" Beware of the allegedly well-meaning friend who subtly (or not so subtly!) infers that he or she knows better than you do. I don't care if your "friend" is a Mensa-certified genius or a world-renowned therapist; anyone who uses your vulnerability as an opportunity to assert superiority is an energy vampire. Friends are there to support your emotional connection to your true self. People who seem impatient with your challenges may have an urgent need to "fix" your problems so that the problems you are grappling with don't remind them of their own vulnerability.

One of the main goals of building a vital support group is to enhance your ability to trust yourself and others. We all benefit from frank feedback that enhances our perception of reality. One word of warning: beware of developing an addiction to the advice of any one person — particularly an addiction to "experts." When we are playing our role, we are often operating from fear. When you are reacting from fear it can seem difficult to trust your own judgment in important matters. However, trusting yourself is perhaps the most important skill you can develop in the service of your success.

While I've always known that it's important to have a healthy support network, the importance of this was reinforced when I made my transition from being an executive to being an executive coach. During my Wall Street career, there were times when it felt like I was surviving emotional guerrilla warfare. Like most of my professional peers, I developed a personal network of cronies to blow off steam with. For years I was the type of person my friends would meet after work or call on the weekends to share grisly anecdotes about the latest interoffice affair or to analyze their passive-aggressive mother. However, for some of these "friends," feeling anxious wasn't a situation, it was a lifestyle.

Once I began the therapeutic training I needed to become an executive coach, I was doing internships in which I would sometimes see

People's experiences change as their positions relative to one another are transformed.

— **Salvador Minuchin**

It's so clear that you have to cherish everyone. I think that's what I get from these older black women, that every soul is to be cherished, that every flower is to bloom.

— Alice Walker

eight to ten emotionally troubled clients in one day. I quickly began to realize that I was going to need to start sorting out the friends who were giving me energy from those that were draining me, or I'd never survive.

Over time I learned to make a concerted effort to nurture my friendships with people who were positive and caring and who showed up for important moments in my life. Part of this process involved setting boundaries with people I cared about who, while they were caring people, tended to be "takers" emotionally. We all want to be there when our friends need us, but it's important to make sure that the energy exchange in your important friendships is balanced. Remember, the more you understand group energy the more you realize that you become like the people with whom you surround yourself.

Many people are so well trained at giving their power away that they don't even realize they are doing it when their role kicks in. I've had many experiences with anxious people who were eager to pay anyone who would tell them what to do. People who feel unable to trust themselves when it comes to the most important decisions in their lives often search frantically for advice from others. When you are considering making any expert a part of your support team, make sure that his or her goal is to help you learn to trust yourself.

Now that you're beginning to understand that some of your most powerful assets are the friends and colleagues who support your ability to nurture your authentic self, it's time to consider the most powerful ways you can use the input from those you trust. The next exercise is designed to help you take in feedback emotionally as well as intellectually to get the fullest sense of how you can be more effective in your on-the-job relationships.

In doing the Influence Chart, you got an initial sense of your level of personal influence within your department. While that exercise has given you valuable insights into areas for improvement, to assess your interpersonal effectiveness from a more intuitive perspective, you also need to consider peer feedback. This feedback will help you learn to shift energy patterns, thereby helping you to advance professionally.

I often ask clients, "If I were to stop your boss in the hall and ask him or her to describe you in three or four words, what do you think those words would be? Would they be complimentary or critical? It always amazes me how many eyes widen at this question, because many of my clients have never considered the impression they are making on others from quite this stark a perspective. This is unfortunate, since in many companies decisions about who to promote and what to pay them are often powerfully influenced by the "sound bite" you create in the minds of others and the way you are casually described by them.

One critical thing to consider in managing the way others experience you personally and professionally is the way others feel about themselves after interacting with you. Do you leave others feeling appreciated and intellectually supported, or criticized and undermined? Many people under pressure become so intent on defending their position that they forget the impression they are making on others as they defend themselves. I frequently remind people that the goal in business and in life is not necessarily to prove to other people that you are smart. The goal is to prove to other people that *they* are smart for working with or knowing you.

As I've already mentioned, most of us are masterful at keeping ourselves from knowing what we would prefer not to know about ourselves. In my experience, you can have emotional revelations at offsite management meetings, you can produce 360-degree feedback reports, and you can talk to an executive until you are blue in the face, but nobody is capable of taking in challenging feedback until two key criteria are met.

We can do no great things — only small things with great love.

— **Mother Teresa**

First, you must have sufficient emotional resilience to take in critical feedback from others. When you are without the proper internal and external support, challenging feedback can trigger a series of mental defense mechanisms that automatically nullify the validity of the feedback. Frequently, a person then makes a series of swift judgments while pointing the finger of blame at the first easy target.

If you have done your exercises in the first two stages, you now have firsthand experience with the sophisticated mental fire walls that the best of us have created to protect ourselves from the unwanted "constructive criticism" of others. To relax these defenses enough to take in challenging feedback that may help us, we must feel reasonably secure in our ability both to trust ourselves and to trust the people offering the feedback. Large organizations waste huge sums of money when they make the dismissive assumption, "Well, of course our employees trust the feedback they are getting from the firm, and they will change their behavior accordingly — after all, we *pay* them!"

Second, in a business context (or any context, for that matter) you must be able to rationalize how acting on this feedback can be in your long-term best interests. Sadly, many organizations find it much easier to generate criticism than to foster methods for helping people actually assimilate this sort of information constructively. Thus, problems are created when an insensitively delivered review suggesting few meaningful steps to take to enhance his or her success leaves an employee struggling to find ways to stay motivated.

A wise man knows everything, a shrewd one, everybody.

— Anonymous

The next exercise, Using the Group's Feedback, can help you put together a successful strategic plan for job advancement. As you do this work, please bear in mind that the criticism that others in your group have of your performance and your interpersonal style may be projections of their own shortcomings. Even so, this doesn't necessarily negate the information. In fact, it may offer vital clues to the less conscious emotions driving those you work with.

Also note that the shortcomings in your performance that others are eager to point out may very well be the flipside of the personality characteristics that make you effective in your job. I've frequently been called in to work with brilliant managers who are given negative reviews because their interpersonal style with both peers and subordinates was described as impatient and dismissive. These same men and women are great at fighting for their departments' priorities and confronting substandard performance. Nobody is asking you to throw out the baby with the bathwater; try not to confuse having areas for improvement pointed out with having your strengths negated. At the same time, bear in mind that "good" is the enemy of "best." Just because your weaknesses are the dark side of your strengths doesn't mean you're going to lose your top performance skills by addressing them. The role you play may warn you that if you don't yell constantly and rule by fear, people will walk all over you. Your authentic self knows better.

EXERCISE:

USING THE GROUP'S FEEDBACK

If you have copies of any performance evaluations or reviews done on you in the past few years, it would be helpful to read them over in preparation for doing this exercise. You will also need your notes from your work with the Influence Chart. Finally, you will need to identify one person from your support network whom you both trust emotionally and respect intellectually to do the last part of this exercise.

Find an hour of uninterrupted time when you can reflect on the following scenarios and answer the accompanying questions.

Reflect on a time when a friend has confronted you about how they were disappointed with your behavior. This may be an ongoing complaint from your spouse or a conflict you had with one of your peers or longtime friends.

1. How did you respond to the other person in this situation? Did your interaction help you clarify your physiological reactions, or did it cause you to suppress them?
2. How do you think your response to the other person made him or her feel?
3. From the perspective of your authentic self, if you could translate your feelings and physiological reactions into words, what would those words be?
4. Do these words reflect the perspective of the role you play or the perspective of your authentic self?

*Be kind,
for everyone you meet
is fighting a hard battle.*
— **Plato**

Reflect on your reaction to someone in the workplace with whom you experience ongoing emotional conflict. This conflict may or may not have been explicitly addressed between the two of you; for example, it may have been with someone who cut you down in an important meeting but with whom you have never discussed the issue.

1. How did you respond to the other person in this situation? Did your interaction help you clarify your physiological reactions, or did it cause you to suppress them?

2. How do you think the way you responded to this person made him or her feel?

3. From the perspective of your authentic self, if you could translate your feelings and physiological reactions into words, what would those words be?

4. Do these words reflect the perspective of the role you play or the perspective of your authentic self?

After reading over your recent reviews and making some notes to yourself about what your boss considers areas for improvement, answer the following:

1. What are the three major areas in which others seem to think I should improve?

2. What is the reaction of the role I play to this feedback?

3. What is the reaction of my authentic self to this feedback?

4. Do I agree with this feedback? Why or why not?

5. Are there any recurring behavior patterns, triggered by my role rather than my authentic self, that others are picking up on?

6. What can I learn about the perspective and emotional needs of others from this feedback?

Take a short break, and then reflect on the following three points to discuss with a trusted member of your support network:

1. The three main areas where others seem to criticize you the most

2. What it would mean to your ongoing sense of self and your value system if any of these criticisms were valid

3. Why you choose to accept or reject this feedback from others

Now it's time to make a dinner date with a trusted member of your support group to discuss the three points above. A word of warning

Half the harm that is done in this world is due to people who want to feel important . . . they do not mean to do harm . . . they are absorbed in an endless struggle to think well of themselves.

— T. S. Eliot

here: be sure to do this exercise with someone with whom you feel emotionally safe. Most of us are in serious denial about how tender we are emotionally and how much we want to please others to get ahead and fit in. Pick someone who is gentle and nonjudgmental. If you can't find someone like that in your current support network, it's time to cultivate some new friendships! In the meantime, you can also do this exercise with a coach, priest, rabbi, or therapist who has sufficient understanding of your work environment to separate the personal from the professional issues as they come up. Whomever you choose, it is vital that you get validation and feedback to complete this exercise. This exercise is about interacting with others as genuinely as possible, and one way to do this is to work on your ability to take in information from those you trust, especially when their perspective differs from yours.

Many people have found that this type of conversation has dramatically enhanced the level of intimacy and trust they have with the people they chose for these discussions. Don't be surprised if your trusted friend ends up doing this exercise right along with you, since these are issues we all grapple with as we try to enhance our ability to work effectively with others.

If we worry too much about ourselves, we won't have time for others.

— **Mother Teresa**

Steven, an investment banker, had been sent for coaching by his firm's CEO because, in spite of his skill with clients, his colleagues consistently complained about his gruff and dismissive interpersonal style. Steven admitted that he had enjoyed the initial stages of coaching much more than he had expected but that he thought the process was paying far better dividends in his marriage than it was in his department. It wasn't until the Interaction Stage of the process that Steven began to understand the power of getting in touch with his feelings and his physiological responses to tense situations in expanding his awareness of the dynamic he was creating with others at work. Steven reported that Using the Group's Feedback helped him react constructively to feedback that previously he would have dismissed.

STEVEN

"The personal situation that came to mind with this exercise was the ongoing debate I have with my wife about speaking to her in my 'business voice.' This exercise started spontaneously when Leslie, who constantly complains that for the first couple of hours after I come home from the office I'm virtually impossible to deal with, started to argue with me. Basically, when she begins complaining, it's such a turnoff that if I wasn't in a bad mood to begin with, her suggestion that I am is enough to make me that way!

"However, in the spirit of doing this exercise, I tried coming home and focusing less on Leslie and more on what was going on inside of me. That was amazing! I could still see Leslie's mouth moving and I knew that a series of criticisms were pouring forth, but my attention went to how shallow my breathing had become. I realized that my teeth were clenching, and so were my fists. When I tried to turn this into words, my mind went blank. All I could manage to do was let the storm of her anger pass, which it did rather quickly when I didn't egg her on, and then wait for some quiet time later in the evening to try and put the episode into perspective.

"As I faced off with the first question from this assignment, the showdown with Leslie was fresh in my mind. I shut my eyes, focused on my breathing, and really tried to see what words I associated with the physical tension that had gripped me when I walked through the front door. At first, all I could focus on was what seemed like a barking dog. Then, I realized that *I* was doing the barking. I had a memory of myself yelling, 'You can't say that to me!... How dare you!... I'll show you who's stupid!' Suddenly I realized that this internal barking was my recurring fantasy that I could finally stand up to my dad for the way he criticized and bullied me all the time when I was a kid. I couldn't believe this stuff was finding another way to come up in my life! I thought that, when I'd realized that this was a factor, I was through with

If we could read the secret history of our enemies, we would find in each man's life a sorrow and a suffering enough to disarm all hostility.

— Henry Wadsworth Longfellow

it. I had no idea how many ways my role of being a bully had sneaked up on me and driven my actions.

"I also realized that the way I habitually reacted to Leslie when I felt threatened in this type of situation probably left her feeling misunderstood and hurt. As I worked through this exercise, it was tough to admit that I had been pretty self-centered in the way I had responded to her. I might as well have been saying to her, 'I feel exhausted and anxious, and who cares how *you* feel! It's time for *me* to matter for a change!' The humbling part of this was she loves me and she never deserves this kind of response. Unfortunately, when these feelings have gotten triggered in the past, she gets blasted just because she's there.

"I just sat there for a minute, stunned. I was really having one of those below-the-neck discoveries you talk about. Now I understand what you meant about nobody else being able to help us be our true selves. Leslie had figured out what was going on with me years ago, and she probably tried to bring it to my attention at least once a week. All that did was piss me off and make that role I play of the bully kick in harder than ever. I'd often wondered why we'd wasted so much time in our coaching sessions dealing with feelings rather than negotiating tactics. Now I understand there's no other way I would have realized the importance of what was going on inside of me on my own.

"The professional questions were a lot easier to deal with than I had anticipated because I was still emotionally stunned by my reaction to the first part of the exercise. I kept being distracted by how scared I was about letting Leslie know she was right about a lot of things. I'd given her so much grief, I figured this would be open season for her to spend the rest of our lives together saying, 'I told you so.'

"I managed to focus, and, as I glanced over the results from my latest performance review, I soon had several images of my behavior in recent meetings that I was less than proud of dancing through my head. I'd yawn loudly, go in and out of the room repeatedly, and say things in an exaggeratedly sarcastic tone of voice when I thought people weren't getting to the point fast enough. As I thought about this, I realized that that was exactly the way my dad responded to me

Whatever you may be sure of, be sure of this — that you are dreadfully like other people.

— James Russell Lowell

when I was a kid, and it made me feel awful! When I focused on the sensations in my body, I realized that this obnoxious role got triggered whenever I was anxious that we were going to miss a deadline or that we were wasting valuable time. So much for frustration tolerance!

"What was even more humbling was that I remembered going over the results from my review with my boss a few months ago, and all I had to say was that the other members of my department were a bunch of 'whiny babies' who didn't understand how to focus on the bottom line!

"It was tough for me to consider how insulted some of my colleagues had probably been by my dismissive behavior. Once again, I wasn't considering how I might be making them feel; I had been too absorbed in my own feelings.

"I finished the rest of the questions, and went down to the kitchen to take a break. Leslie gave me a tight smile when she saw me, and turned away. I took her by the hand, gave her a big hug, and told her how sorry I was that I'd been such a grouch. At first, she was suspicious. That almost made me mad at her all over again, but I kept focusing on my breathing and what was going on in my body, and I realized I was just afraid of not being good enough. When I thought about it calmly, I couldn't blame her for being a bit suspicious after all I'd put her through.

I observe myself and I come to know others.

— Lao-tzu

"Leslie and I talked for a couple of hours that night, and I was completely surprised by her reaction to my apology. I expected her to be hostile and critical, but she was warm and loving — somehow she managed to forgive me for my bad behavior more easily than I was able to forgive myself!

"I decided to do the feedback part of the exercise with this guy, Paul, who had been a friend of mine for years and who used to work with me at another bank. Paul knows me professionally as well as personally, so he's pretty well suited to give me a realistic appraisal of whether or not I'm out of line.

"When I asked him to be frank with me about whether or not he thought I was too abrasive at the office, his response really shocked me.

I'd tried to get Paul to join our firm a few years ago, but he had refused, saying he got a lucrative counteroffer that he couldn't turn down. During our discussion, Paul admitted that one reason he hadn't taken the job was that he was afraid working with me would ruin our friendship. One of the key reasons he worried about this was because he said he didn't know how to talk to me when I lost it. Paul looked so anxious while he was telling me this that I had to keep reassuring him that I was fine. I'm pretty powerful in our industry, and as Paul and I talked I realized there weren't many people who had the guts to tell me what they really thought of me. Of course, until recently, I hadn't really had the guts to listen anyway."

Each thought,
each action in the sunlight
of awareness,
becomes sacred.

— **Thich Nhat Hanh**

Your ability to have a breakthrough experience with this exercise is usually a good test of how much progress you have actually made in being your authentic self. The fact of the matter is that although most of us have huge blind spots about our own vulnerabilities, we usually have mercilessly sharp insight into the shortcomings of others. This means that while your colleagues' perspectives of reality may be driven by the skewed values of our material culture, there are usually some insights in there that are well worth noting.

People tend to learn a lesson in this exercise that is critical in moving forward successfully with the Authentic Career Process: emotional honesty is infectious. No matter how challenging it may be to come to terms with aspects of your behavior that are less than perfect, when you really try to be honest you often find that others are solidly on your side. Emotional honesty is the foundation of genuine connection with others.

Emotional honesty is also critical to profitability in business. One team of senior executives I worked with had everyone in the group do a version of this exercise. When we were going over the results, these highly quantitative executives became so absorbed in the implications of this work that they actually calculated the hourly cost of having highly paid managers unable to concentrate because of thoughtless behavior and poor communication. Then they went on to calculate the "watercooler hours" of lost productivity because the staff reporting to these managers became more focused on gossiping about the childish conflict between their superiors than they were on their jobs. The final blow came when the group calculated the opportunity cost of losing an important contract to a competitor whose productivity was not held hostage by childish bickering and emotional agendas between key managers. The grand total from this example turned out to be a loss in the millions of dollars due to poor communication skills and to turning a blind eye to the importance of the human element. At the end of the seminar, this team had dubbed this work the "Titanic Exercise." This is because the interpersonal conflicts that take place when people are unconscious about how they are affecting each other are only the tip of the iceberg in business; the actual costs of these problems can often be much greater than they appear on the surface.

Taking the risk of discussing your professional vulnerabilities with a trusted friend helps you to strengthen your ability to trust yourself. The final chapter of the Interaction Stage is designed to help you build on this foundation of personal integrity to cultivate skills you can use in achieving your professional goals.

Really great men have a curious feeling that the greatness is not in them, but through them. And they see something divine in every other man.

— John Ruskin

Much has been written about the importance of cultivating a persuasive interpersonal style in business. What has rarely been discussed openly is the primal level of frustration and the toxic energy produced when people feel interpersonally blocked. In the Emotional Ownership Stage, you learned how suppressing uncomfortable feelings produces physiological reactions. In the Interaction Stage, you learn how the level of emotional honesty between people influences the energy that is created between people when they interact.

To interact with others persuasively, you must understand the role that energy plays in interpersonal relationships. When you communicate with others, you are exchanging energy as well as information.

Frequently, I have worked with executives who are outraged when others who don't seem to work as hard as they do or to have as much industry experience are promoted over them. "It's not fair!" wails the executive who seethes in frustration as he or she watches a less experienced colleague who has won a coveted promotion gaily chatting up the boss night after night. Such frustration results from the belief that hard work alone should be sufficient to ensure prosperity and recognition. But, especially in a competitive corporate environment, it simply doesn't work this way. An equal amount of effort must be put into cultivating meaningful professional relationships.

By this point in the Authentic Career Process, you should have a clearer understanding of the way the pressures from your workplace environment can influence whether you are being authentic or reverting to the role you play under pressure. Nothing triggers the temptation to operate from the role we internalized from our family more than a good old-fashioned power struggle at our jobs.

Power struggles are rampant, especially in corporate America. This is because many people are suffering from "spiritual anorexia" and an

CHAPTER 9

Remaining True to Yourself Under Pressure

inability to connect with the power of their authentic selves. Because of this deficiency they have to suck power from those around them to keep going. Let's face it: you're going to have to get energy from somewhere. If you aren't able to replenish your energy from within, you're going to have to get it from without. On a more minor level, in the external search for energy, you may drink a little too much coffee or eat a few too many candy bars to feel "up." While this works temporarily, you sacrifice your ability to stay in tune with your body when you habitually energize yourself with caffeine or sugar.

Yet even people who are mindful of keeping their bodies in tune can fall into destructive patterns in an attempt to replenish their energy when they don't know how to find it within. The more extreme examples of the external search for power are those who feel the need to mentally dominate and manipulate others to get their way. We see it — and *feel it* — in corporate America every day.

Do unto others as you would have others do unto you.

—The Golden Rule

Many people don't understand the inherent power of being true to themselves under pressure. Like many of our abilities, getting in touch with the authentic self counts most under pressure. Most of us can interact with others professionally, negotiate persuasively, and even remain mindful of the bigger picture when everything is going smoothly. However, it's when we feel pressured by undermining colleagues, looming deadlines, and diminished resources that being authentic *really* counts.

The ability to be authentic and to replenish our energy from within is vital in work environments where ethical questions are becoming increasingly complex. When we look within, we remember that there are an infinite number of solutions to any challenge. This realization gives us the confidence to consider all sides of a complex question. When we are playing a role, we are only able to see the aspects of a complex question that our role is comfortable with, so the range of solutions we are able to envision narrows. Outstanding interpersonal skills and the ability to navigate the currents of workplace politics successfully can be learned.

Mastering the interpersonal skills you need to achieve your professional goals doesn't require that you be born with innate charisma or that you come from a supportive family that has celebrated your every success. What you do need is the willingness to face the fact that inter-acting persuasively with others is a skill and that you will need to work on this skill if you want to get ahead.

The work in the final chapter of the Interaction Stage is designed to help you use your enhanced self-awareness, your mind-body con-nection, and your understanding of group energy to shift the balance of power in your favor as you interact with others. This exercise may look simple the first time you read through it. However, the dynamics that you will experience when you do this work can have a profound impact on your professional success.

A loving person lives in a loving world. A hostile person lives in a hostile world: Everyone you meet is your mirror.

— Ken Keyes Jr.

EXERCISE:

THE DRESS REHEARSAL FOR THE AUTHENTIC SELF

This exercise will help you use your role-playing ability consciously so that you can adhere to your true values rather than unconsciously play-ing a part under pressure. This conscious role-playing is designed to help you react to professional challenges from the perspective of your authentic self through rehearsing this behavior with members of your support network. This work helps you cultivate the skill of being more fully aware of the energetic exchange taking place when you communicate with others in the workplace.

Choose a member of your support network to work with on this role-play exercise. You and your friend (some clients do this with their spouse) will role-play a professional challenge that you will consciously respond to both from the perspective of the role you play and then from the perspective of your authentic self.

This exercise consists of four parts. The first two are the back-ground work you will do before meeting with your partner to make your role-playing as effective as possible. The last two will require you to find an evening when you can spend some uninterrupted time with your partner.

A certain naiveté is a prerequisite to all learning. A certain optimism is a prerequisite to all action.

— George Leonard

ACCESSING YOUR EMOTIONAL MEMORY

Think of an emotionally charged situation at work when you were playing your role. It can be any type of power struggle or conflict that was particularly challenging for you. Try to remember as many specific details as possible. There is a famous saying, "the genius is in the details," and this is particularly true in understanding the role that timing and context play in workplace interactions.

Write out your memory of this situation, paying particular attention to the following details:

Mindfulness must be engaged. Once there is seeing, there must be acting. Otherwise, what is the use of seeing?

— Thich Nhat Hanh

1. Where was I when this interaction took place?
2. What triggered this workplace conflict?
3. What time of day was it?
4. Were there other people present? If so, what was their reaction to this conflict?
5. Was I able to identify the dominant emotions I was feeling at the time? If not, why not? Am I able to identify the dominant emotions I am feeling now?
6. How would I describe the energy that was created between the people present in this interaction?

TRACKING YOUR PHYSICAL RESPONSES

We convey all our internal reactions in some manner through our physical responses to others. Even people who have learned to appear impassive in tense situations, much like professional gamblers, frequently convey by their silence and their lack of expression that they are furiously assessing a situation internally because they are unsure of how to respond.

Furthermore, the physical sensations we experience and may even unconsciously display in our interactions with others may be mirroring vital information about what's going on with those around us. Often one of the most powerful and primal methods of communication is called "emotional induction." Many people aren't fully conscious of the way that inducing feelings in others is a vital form of communication. For example, a common house cat expresses anxiety by arching its back and hissing, thus communicating its anxiety by inducing this feeling in those present. Similarly, an edgy employee anxious about meeting a deadline can induce this anxiety in others by glancing anxiously at his or her watch, fidgeting, and responding in terse monosyllables.

Thus it is vital to remember as clearly as possible your physical responses to a challenging workplace conflict, since these are a rich source of information about what you were sensing about others — and what you were conveying about yourself.

1. How conscious was I of the sensations in my body during this situation?
2. What information can I add to my memory of this situation by remembering what I was experiencing physically?
3. How conscious was I of my breathing during the interaction? Was my breath deep and relaxed, or shallow and anxious?
4. What did my breath tell me about my internal reactions?
5. What was my vocal tone? How rapidly did I speak?
6. What was the connection between the physical sensations I experienced and the energy created?
7. How did this behavior reflect the values of the role I play under pressure? How did this behavior reflect the values of my authentic self?

A hurtful act is the transference to others of the degradation which we bear in ourselves.

— Simone Weil

Trust only movement. Life happens at the level of events, not of words. Trust movement.

—Alfred Adler

FOCUSING YOUR IMAGINATION

Now you are ready to role-play this situation with your chosen partner. Using the notes you made in the first two sections, explain the conflict to your partner in as much detail as possible. Then role-play this situation, re-creating your behavior in this scene as vividly as possible, by having your partner play the part of the person who triggered the conflict.

After you have done this role-play, switch parts. This time you should play the part of the person with whom you experienced a power struggle, and your partner should play you. Bear in mind that your partner should play you as you are when you are acting from the perspective of your role. When you have acted out both sides of this power struggle, discuss the following questions with your partner:

1. What new information did I discover by acting out both sides of this power struggle?
2. Do I have more insight into what might have been motivating the person I was in conflict with now that I have role-played his or her side of this conflict?
3. What insight can my partner give me about what I convey to others when I am playing my role under pressure?

BEING IN TOUCH WITH THE AUTHENTIC SELF

You are now going to role-play the same professional challenge with your partner, but this time you are going to react "as if" you had been in touch with your authentic self during this conflict. "Acting as if" is a powerful technique that was developed by the famous Russian drama coach Konstantin Stanislavsky for accessing one's emotional memory and focusing the imagination. Stanislavsky taught his pupils that by being mindful of their internal physical responses in a given situation, they would also influence the emotions evoked in the external world.

It may seem ironic to cite the work of one of the founders of method acting to help you *stop* playing a role and start being more authentic. Let me explain further. Stanislavsky taught his students that their physical actions were the "inner key" to evoking authentic emotional responses from the less-conscious parts of their being. While clients have frequently told me that this exercise seemed simple when they first read through it, the act of consciously tracking and changing their physical responses to interpersonal situations helped them to "wake up" and realize when they were unconsciously playing a role that was not serving their long-term professional goals.

In this part of the exercise, you will be "acting as if" you had the flexibility to see from the perspective of your ideal self. This type of flexibility and emotional honesty is only possible when you do not need to play the emotional games that are second nature to you when you are playing a role in a challenging interpersonal situation. The process of "acting as if" helps you to deal with the powerful (and frequently semiconscious) triggers that drive you to play this limiting role under pressure.

After role-playing this challenge from the perspective of your authentic self, reflect on the following questions with your partner:

1. How does my body language and my posture change when I am operating from the perspective of my authentic self?
2. How does the tempo with which I react to others shift when I am operating from my authentic self?
3. Do I experience any changes in my breathing or the sensations I am aware of in my body when I am operating from my authentic self?
4. Do I assign the same meaning to the behavior of others when I am operating from my authentic self as I do when I am playing my role?
5. Are there any key differences in the energy created between me and others when I am seeing from the perspective of my authentic self as opposed to when I am playing my role?

After you have completed this exercise, take some time to write down the main points of your discussion with your partner about the different ways that you responded to this challenge.

Big ideas are so hard to recognize, so fragile, so easy to kill. Don't forget that, all of you who don't have them.

— John Elliott Jr.

Sally works for an international shipping firm. She came in for coaching when she found out that, owing to a reorganization among the senior managers at her firm, she would be reporting to a supervisor whom she didn't respect or trust. Doing the Dress Rehearsal for the Authentic Self exercise helped give Sally some valuable perspective so that she was able to take responsibility for her side of this power struggle and to prevent this troubled relationship from sabotaging her career.

SALLY

"I've been really confused about how to express how furious I am over having to report to my current boss, Ken. I want to resign over this, but my husband is a high school teacher, and we have a daughter to support. We really need the income my job provides.

"I had an extremely uncomfortable lunch with Ken after I found out I would be reporting to him — so uncomfortable that I ended up pretending to be sick so I could leave early and just get away. Basically, in my attempt to be honest, I told Ken that I didn't trust him and didn't see any reason why I ever would. Since Ken doesn't have the authority to fire me, but senior management insists that I report to him, we have a power struggle extraordinaire.

"I was tempted to play my role immediately when Ken started discussing our reporting relationship. The minute he mentioned this, my mind began to whirl with memories of what a jerk he had been in the past and nightmares of how awful my life could be in the future working for him. The best word to describe the energy created by the two of us coming together that day is *toxic*. In fact, it was so bad that a couple near us who looked like they had been trying to have a relaxing lunch actually moved to get away from us.

"The physical sensations I identified while doing this exercise were powerful. The more upset I got, the shallower my breath got and the more my stomach began to churn. After a while, my breath got so shallow that I began to feel like I would suffocate. It felt like the more toxic the energy got between us, the harder it was for me to breathe. This difficulty catching my breath is the same physical response I have had recently trying to get my dismissive parents to recognize me as an adult.

"I decided to role-play this uncomfortable lunch meeting with Judy, one of the friends from my Support Group Inventory. She and I have been in the same industry for years. As a successful business-woman who has had problems with a couple of bosses in the course of

her own career, Judy understands my challenges when it comes to dealing with Ken both personally and professionally.

"I tried to stay in touch with what was going on in my body as I
allowed myself to re-create what had happened to me in this meeting
with Ken. My breath got shallow and my voice started to get shrill as
I was role-playing this scene with Judy. As my voice rose while Judy
and I went at it, I realized that the lack of control I felt in this situation was making me act crazy. Even though part of me knew that Judy
wasn't really Ken, and that we were just playing out a scene together,
once we got going I found that I wasn't letting Judy get a word in edge-
wise. My face was turning red, and I realized at one point that I was
clenching my fist under the table.

"Judy told me that, while she was playing the part of Ken, she felt
devalued and criticized. She described the energy created by this scene
as oppressive and told me she was feeling slightly nauseated, even
though she knew we were only role-playing. She told me that it
seemed like I was obsessed with Ken's past behavior and totally unwilling to give him a chance in his new position.

"This exercise helped me become more consciously aware that I actually was unwilling to give Ken a chance as my manager. However, what's
more important, Judy's feedback helped me realize that I was telegraph-
ing this negativity to Ken even when I was trying to watch my words.

"When Judy and I switched roles, I was amazed at how my perspective of the situation changed when I was playing Ken's part. Judy
had promised me that she was going to portray my behavior as accu-
rately as possible so that I could get a feel for what other people experienced with me. As Judy did her best imitation of me, I realized that
I was terrified of this shrill, anxious woman sitting across from me.
As I tried to describe the energy, it felt like being slapped in the face
with a tidal wave of fury. Even though I knew we were just acting,
when Judy started acting out my anger it got pretty scary.

"By the time we got to the third part of the exercise where I was
going to 'act as if' I were operating from my authentic self, I wasn't
sure what to expect. I remembered what you'd told me in our coaching

*The test of a man or
woman's breeding is how
they behave in a quarrel.*

— George Bernard Shaw

*My greatest weapon
is mute prayer.*

— Mahatma Gandhi

*It is our lack of love for
ourselves that inhibits our
compassion toward others.
If we make friends with
ourselves, then there is no
obstacle to opening our
hearts and minds to others.*

— Pema Chödrön

session about the authentic self being 'in the moment' and about remembering to observe more and react less.

"As I tried to stay in touch with the messages I was getting from my body, particularly the pace of my breathing, it dawned on me that it was my pride that kept me from admitting to myself that I was afraid that Ken had the power to torpedo my career. Admitting to myself that he was in a more powerful position than I was made me feel like a loser. As I stayed with my breath to find out where in my body this feeling of being a loser was coming from, it brought up all the same uncomfortable sensations I experienced as a child when I realized how I had twisted myself into a pretzel emotionally over the years trying to gain my parents' elusive approval. I was extremely concerned, considering that there might be a parallel between how I reacted to Ken's power in this situation and how I reacted to people who had power over me in general.

"I stayed with my breath and tried to channel my anger and resentment into a simple sentence that would articulate what I wanted. I also tried to consciously diffuse the toxic energy this situation seemed to create so I could minimize some of the intensity. As I stayed focused on my breath, I realized that all I wanted was the chance to do my job without being undermined or politically backstabbed. I found myself looking Judy in the eye while we played this scene and saying in a low, measured voice, 'All I want is the chance to do my job in safety.'

*If you bring forth
what is inside of you,
what you bring forth will
save you. If you don't bring
forth what is inside of you,
what you don't bring
forth will destroy you.*

— Gnostic Gospels

"Judy told me later that everything, from my body language to my tone of voice to the expression on my face had opened up and made me seem more accessible and even more *professional* when I had worked through my internal emotions enough to articulate clearly what I wanted. She also told me that her sense of the energy created between us when I was being true to myself was much less intense, and that the whole scene felt safer.

"That night, as I wrote some notes to myself about what I had experienced doing this work, I realized that the role I played under pressure not only made me unapproachable to others, but it also made it hard for me to be aware of what was going on inside me. I also realized that being aware of the energy I'm creating with others helps me become more conscious of when I slip into my role and how to be more my authentic self."

⁂

In any given interaction we are communicating constantly at a non-verbal level. We forget this at our peril. People sense our intentions on many levels. They may not be consciously aware of exactly what's going on with us, but on some level they get it.

When we are playing our role, we often suppress unwanted emotions. Not only do we cut off access to our inner wisdom when we do this, we also create toxic energy in our interactions with others. Energy is never destroyed. Therefore, negative emotions that are not consciously acknowledged come out in a way that frequently has a powerful impact on those around us. Our workplaces today are filled with examples of energy in action. Often an angry boss can cause her staff to feel angry and disoriented without even raising her voice. Her anger is communicated energetically rather than verbally. Similarly, a person who is repeatedly passed over for promotion may be communicating feelings of worthlessness even though he speaks intelligently and behaves professionally. As you strengthen your connection with your authentic self, you become able to identify the powerful emotions that workplace challenges trigger in you and the energy being created by your interactions. Being in touch with yourself is a prerequisite for shifting the energy in any situation. This is because energy is created in the present moment, and the present moment is also the focus of the authentic self.

As you get used to tuning in to the energy being created in various situations, you will gradually learn how to use this knowledge to diffuse potential conflicts. People who cultivate their awareness eventually learn how to work with the group energy in a workplace culture so that their ambitions are supported rather than undermined. Thus, when it comes to politics on the job, being connected with your true self is a powerful advantage.

You have a good many little gifts and virtues, but there is no need of parading them, for conceit spoils the finest genius. There is not much danger that real talent or goodness will be overlooked long, and the great charm of all power is modesty.

— Louisa May Alcott

We are more anxious to speak than to be heard.

— Henry David Thoreau

Violence is the last refuge
of the incompetent.

— Isaac Asimov

This brings us to the wonderful subject of how to strengthen your connection to your authentic self. The work in this stage has heightened your awareness of the role your emotions play in your interactions with others. Learning to focus your emotional energy in a healthy way is the key to realizing your professional goals without sacrificing your personal power in the process. This enhanced sensitivity to your connection with others also builds the intuitive foundation necessary to proceed successfully to the Integration Stage.

STAGE IV
INTEGRATION

The work you will do in the Integration Stage will help you to build the skills you need to draw confidently on your intuition as a complement to your intellectual abilities. While we all experience flashes of intuition, the exercises in this final section of the Authentic Career Process are designed to help you cultivate the ability to trust your inner knowing more consistently.

Our intuition and our intelligence reinforce each other. We must cultivate our mental flexibility if we hope to use our intuition and our intelligence together. This type of mental flexibility is critical in a complex business climate where we need to be able to grasp all sides of a complex question — not just those sides we are emotionally comfortable with. When we are in touch with our inner knowing, we remember that there are an infinite number of solutions to any professional challenge. However, when our fears lock us into the limited perspective of the role we play, we are unable to envision possibilities that are emotionally challenging. In today's rapidly changing world, cultivating the mind-body awareness that keeps us in touch with the ethical implications and emotional repercussions of business decisions is not just an issue of personal integrity — it is an issue of economic survival.

Learning to trust your inner knowing is the foundation of practical spirituality. Again, please remember that when I use the word *spiritual* in this book, I am referring to an individual's innate connection with his or her authentic nature — and not to the ideology of any mainstream religion. Cultivating practical spirituality helps you naturally to integrate your personal goals with your public responsibilities.

Individuals who adopt a team-oriented approach to success often find that it is in their self-interest to focus on ways that they can support others — not because they are "nice" but because they are aware.

Imagination is more important than knowledge.

— Albert Einstein

People who are aware of their interconnection with others don't turn a blind eye or respond like accepting zombies when they encounter unethical or unprofessional behavior in the day-to-day political jostling for position that takes place in many work environments. This is because those who understand that we are all interconnected know that by not defending their true values, they are eroding their own power.

Many people are amazed by the amount of personal power they unlock as they do this work. People who develop a sophisticated understanding of the way group energy works gradually develop a deeper understanding of how interconnected we all are. They begin to realize that when they are cultivating their authentic talents and pursuing their genuine interests, they begin to exert a more powerful impact on the group energy around them.

The work you will do in this stage will help you to build the confidence you need to trust your inner wisdom. In turn, learning to trust yourself is the foundation for building trusting relationships with others. This stage is divided into three chapters:

There is nothing so secular that it cannot be sacred, and that is one of the deepest messages of the Incarnation.

— Madeline L'Engle

- *Chapter 10: "Learning to Trust Your Inner World."* The first goal of this work is not to cultivate some type of mysterious skill set. Rather, it is about becoming more conscious of a part of your innate human nature. The goal of this work is to help you recognize the ways that messages from your authentic self have already been guiding you throughout your life.

- *Chapter 11: "Using New Tools for Old Challenges."* The second goal of the Integration Stage is to help you use your authentic abilities more consistently. As you practice accessing your inner knowing daily, you gradually learn how to shift into the perspective of your ideal self when faced with challenges and to focus your personal power more consciously.

- *Chapter 12: "Maintaining an Interdependent Perspective."* The work in the final chapter of the Authentic Career Process is designed to help you maintain your commitment to authentic success by integrating your desire for personal gain with your beliefs about your responsibility to others. This work will help you to create a holistic definition of success that helps you draw both on your emotional desires and on the power of your imagination. Integrating your emotions and your imagination is the key not only to helping you achieve your current goals, but also to maintaining an authentic, ongoing commitment to setting new and higher goals for yourself.

The whole of science is nothing more than a refinement of everyday thinking.

— Albert Einstein

By maintaining your commitment to your personal power, not only are you better able to fulfill your personal desires, but you also gradually create a surplus of energy you can use to focus on the needs of others without becoming drained. Many people have used the work in the Integration Stage as a foundation for exploring their own brand of practical spirituality.

Learning to trust the wisdom of the inner self is a spiritual skill. Blind faith has no place in practical spirituality. Religions that demand this blind faith contribute to the rampant confusion between spirituality and religion that keeps many people from cultivating their inner knowing

In many ways, the atheist who shakes his or her fist at the heavens in rage, demanding proof of a loving God, is more spiritually advanced than the terrified religious follower meekly mumbling prayers that he or she doesn't even understand. Why? Because you can't be true to yourself when you give your power away.

Freedom involves the ability to think for ourselves. It involves the ability to trust our own experience and to question the beliefs of others when they don't fit with our understanding. Mental freedom gives birth to independent thinking. In a world of rampant prejudice, opinion manipulation, and biased data selection, we need to cultivate as many independent thinkers as we can if we are going to adapt and survive.

Learning to think for yourself and to trust your inner knowing is the foundation of true success. Trusting your internal wisdom helps you to understand the patterns of your life at a deeper level. It is becoming more and more vital to tap into this knowledge as the expectations of the workplace demand more results, while giving us less time in which to produce them. The ability to key in to our inner wisdom enables many people to produce results in nonlinear time — meaning that they experience insights and become intuitively aware of relationships that would otherwise take hours or weeks of more linear thought to decipher.

Practical spirituality encourages you to question everything. When my clients question their ability to access their spiritual resources, I

CHAPTER 10

Learning to Trust Your Inner World

ask them to do these exercises. The only guide you should trust concerning something this important is your own experience. One of the most fundamental tenets of my coaching philosophy is that you must learn to trust yourself. Don't take it from me that your authentic self is ready and waiting to get into the game. To accept a proposition this big, you should really consider the evidence. The evidence is in your own life.

EXERCISE:

THE MANDALA OF YOUR LIFE

This exercise is going to be reminiscent of the Personal Tree of Life exercise that you did in the Awareness Stage. You may find it helpful to get out many of the same pictures that you used for that exercise. You will also need a stack of note cards, some colored pens, and your journal or laptop.

Genius . . . means little more than the faculty of perceiving in an unhabitual way.

—William James

The first step in creating the Mandala of Your Life is to do a time line of all the important events in your life, in chronological order. To do this time line, indicate the significant events of your life on your note cards, using one card to jot down a sentence that describes each event. If you reflect on your work from past exercises, be sure to consider its emotional importance to you *at the present time.* If all your past relationships with significant others were meaningful in shaping your life, please indicate them. If, from your perspective today, only some of these relationships were significant, then only indicate the ones that apply.

Because the use of visual symbols helps to stimulate intuition, the second step involves taking all the significant events in your life on your note cards and translating them into symbols or pictures. To do this, draw a symbol that represents this life event to you on the back of each card. For example, you can draw a heart for an important anniversary and a dollar sign for an important job opportunity.

If you have photos handy, you can also use pictures to represent significant events. This exercise works just as well when using symbols on note cards, photos, or some combination of the two, as long as you have some visual symbol to indicate the significant moments of your life.

The third step involves laying out all your visual symbols from left to right, in chronological order, so that the story of your life is spread out in pictures before you and you are looking at a linear flow of the significant moments of your life. Some people have so many cards they have to make two or three rows to cover the whole story. That's great — it's the sign of a life rich with experiences.

Now we're going to play with our linear conception of time a little bit. Reverse the order of these cards so that they are flowing backward. As you do this, think of the present moment as your starting point and the development of the ensuing events as stretching into your future rather than coming from your past. Take a minute to note in your journal any insights you may have as you do this. This mental shuffling is to help you get a little more objective about the order in which you usually contemplate your reality.

Now pick out the events that have the most emotional meaning to you at the present moment. They can come from anywhere in the flow, regardless of time. Try not to start with more than five. This may take some sorting, so take your time. When you've picked out the most emotionally meaningful moments of your life, take a moment to jot down a few notes in your journal — just a sentence or two — about why you selected these particular cards.

From this set, pick the one card that from your current perspective represents the most emotionally meaningful moment of your life. Take that card and place it in the center of the other cards. Now arrange the other cards around this card in a rough circle. If an event on another card seems to resonate with a similar energy as the card in the center, or to be related to it in some way, place it a bit closer to

The most beautiful experience we can have is the mysterious. . . . He to whom this emotion is a stranger, who can no longer pause to wonder and stand rapt in awe, is as good as dead.

— Albert Einstein

the center. Those cards that are less emotionally meaningful to you should be in the circle — but a bit farther from the center. When you have done this, step back and take it in. You have now created your mandala.

Take a moment to reflect on the card in the center. Imagine the scene that this card represents as vividly as possible. Now go back to your circle and make any adjustments that feel right to you in arranging the other cards around this card, letting this scene attract other scenes to it. Feel the connections between this central scene and other events in your life from the perspective of your authentic self. Keep arranging and rearranging the cards in your mandala until you get a sense of unity from the pattern you have created.

Now take some time to write in your journal or laptop about the tableau you have created, and reflect on the following questions:

1. What does this visual history tell you about the role that your authentic self has played in your life up to this point?
2. How does this visual history resonate with your deepest desires and sense of purpose today?
3. Pay special attention to the emotional content of all the events in your mandala and their interconnections with one another. What are the beliefs behind these emotions?
4. What patterns connect these emotions and beliefs?
5. Can you identify a central message or sense of purpose from the mandala you have made? (Hint: Don't force yourself to put the answer to this last question into words if it doesn't come easily. Our deeper knowing is not always dependent on language.)

Be sure to give yourself all the time you need for this work. This exercise is a bit like yoga for the spirit; it's better to do it mindfully rather than rapidly.

Susan, a designer, told me that the evening she did the Mandala of Your Life exercise was so special for her that she had to create another card to represent that experience as she was having it.

*The soul
can split the sky in two,
and let the face
of God shine through.*

— Edna St. Vincent Millay

I don't believe; I know.

— Carl Jung

⚜

SUSAN

"I'd actually started doing a time line about the important events in my life a few years ago when I was journaling more regularly. I pulled my old journal out and used my previous notes to do an updated time line on a long roll of computer paper that I could spread across the bedroom floor. Interestingly, I found myself adding my nieces' birthdays to my time line — that was a new one. They've been coming in to the city to spend time with me more and more this year. As I redid this time line, I realized that spending time with them was incredibly important to me emotionally.

"I set out the pictures of important events in my life in the order they had taken place along the top of the time line. By the time I was done, I had a four-foot personal mural spread across my bedroom floor. Where I didn't like the appropriate photo — or where I didn't have one — I drew symbols on cards to represent the event.

"Rearranging these pictures and symbols to look at the events of my life backward was tougher than I had imagined. It brought up some powerful emotions. As I did this, I realized I'd come from this wonderful small-town family where I had people around me all the time and had ended up in a huge city surrounded by millions of people being alone together. I was surprised by how much the longing for a home and family was influencing me emotionally. I realized that if all those ambitious fashion designers I work with had a clue how much I loved shopping at the local mall, because it reminds me of my roots, they'd be shocked.

"Picking out the cards that were most important to me was easier than I thought it would be. Thanks to all that work I'd done on Weeding the Shoulds and spotting the roles I play, I was much less hung up on my image — and much more in touch with my real self. The whole process felt like a meditation as I was going through it. What astounded me, though, was that my most important card was the

The psychological rule says that when a situation is not made conscious, it happens outside, as fate. That is to say, when the individual remains undivided and does not become conscious of his inner contradictions, the world must perforce act out the conflict and be torn into opposite halves.

— Carl Jung

To one who has faith,
no explanation is necessary.
To one without faith, no
explanation is possible.

— Saint Thomas Aquinas

picture of me with my nieces in front of the skating rink at Rockefeller Center. I realized that this picture was powerful for me because it represented the energy I got from being able to help them understand their power to create anything they wanted in their lives. Showing my nieces around the city that day and sharing my experiences with them had helped me feel my own creative power intensely.

"As I created my circle with the other cards around this one, my authentic self was in full force. The energy of nurturing others was the energy of 'home' for me — but my home was much bigger now than the small town I'd grown up in. I realized why it was so important to me to mother the young women who worked with me in fashion and to stand up for the importance of inner beauty in an industry that can be exhaustingly superficial at times. I felt an incredible surge of power as I realized that my authentic self had been guiding my path every step of the way — even when my doubts and insecurities about not being married with kids drained my energy at times.

"I got an incredible surge of gratitude from this exercise. I could see how some of the chance meetings and opportunities in my life had landed me in a position where I could use my love of beauty and my talents in ways that were healing for me and for others at the same time."

Life is not a problem
to be solved,
but a mystery to be lived.

— Thomas Merton

Susan's experience with this exercise shows that most of us don't give ourselves nearly enough credit for the power we already have to create our own reality. You simply can't escape the fact that you are living your own truth, whatever your circumstances may be. Many of us try to live the truths of people who are important to us — our parents, our supervisors, our friends, our teachers — but our authentic energy almost always gets blocked in this process. Many of us who have been steeped in self-doubt because we cannot live up to the ideals of others frequently stumble across the realization that this "failure" may be the source of our greatest success.

At its essence, practical spirituality is pretty simple. That's why kids are such a spiritual inspiration. Spirituality is about freedom, spontaneity, and connection to the core of our true natures. It is about trusting ourselves, not leading our lives according to others. Cultivating our spiritual resources is the foundation of true freedom.

Your work in cultivating your mind-body awareness up to this point has helped you to realize that your emotions trigger your memories and, in turn, your memories organize your associations. This is how we create the wonderful shifting patterns of associations that we use to form our perspective of reality at any given moment.

The road to authentic power is often anything but smooth. As you learn to transcend the limits you have placed on your mental and emotional freedom in the past, you continuously discover new ways that those old values and limiting core beliefs test your mental flexibility.

Mediocrity knows nothing higher than itself, but talent instantly recognizes genius.

— Arthur Conan Doyle

CHAPTER 11

Using New Tools for Old Challenges

Many of us have been taught to look outside ourselves for intellectual information to help us deal with personal and professional challenges. As helpful as the advice of experts can be, the wisdom of others should be used as a sounding board that helps us clarify our inner knowing. We are giving our power away when we use the advice of our consultants, counselors, priests, rabbis, and so on as a substitute for going within.

There is nothing new about the concepts of cultivating our inner knowing, sharpening our capacity for critical thinking, and focusing our desires. Many of these concepts draw on ancient wisdom. When I discuss using new tools for old challenges, the "newness" I am referring to comes from the assertion that cultivating your inner knowing can be as important as, say, a good cash-flow statement when dealing with career challenges.

Meditation is one of the simplest and most straightforward tools for cultivating your inner knowing. Today many people are fascinated with the benefits of meditation because, at some level, they realize that their intuition is simply an extension of their physical senses being more tuned in.

Understanding the power of silence is vital to focusing your personal power. In the safety of silence your authentic self can spread out and make itself known. In the safety of silence your inner knowing brings joyous discoveries, unexpected solutions, and gifts of wisdom. Your connection to the divinity within and without is strengthened in silence. One reason that so many people are obsessed with material gain in this culture is that we are so bombarded by artificial stimuli that we are drowning out the voice of our true selves. When you look into the eyes of a five-year-old who has been exposed to so many visual images of violence that his natural innocence has evaporated before he even starts to develop social skills, it breaks your heart.

The culture of materialism is working hard to commercialize and complicate many simple spiritual concepts. "Why do I find it so hard to meditate?" harried clients complain. "Why aren't I more sensitive, more intuitive, more psychic?" whisper discouraged executives who have been furtively reading the metaphysical literature that is cascading from bookstore shelves into briefcases. As the media obediently fill our demand for fantasy in a world where reality frequently feels like a treadmill, our definitions of God have been hyped and commercialized along with everything else. Movies, television programs, and reams of literature that skillfully blend tidbits of ancient wisdom with New Age platitudes have pervaded our cultural consciousness. We are fed the hope that if we "visualize success" we can manifest our dreams magically without having to deal with cranky bosses and long commutes.

Sadly, the key ingredient that is often left out of this imaginative brew is the fact that the heart of spiritual growth involves focusing more on what we have to give than on what we hope to get. This means that an overpriced course on "stroking your psychic sensitivity," when pursued as a skill to enhance your sales numbers, may be a great place to find an open-minded date, but it's unlikely to help mute the demands of your job.

Meditation and self-reflection are natural processes for any human being. In the initial stages of coaching, I find myself gently reminding clients that if they could just find ten minutes a day to sit quietly with themselves, it would change their lives. Often I will ask clients who are particularly reluctant to slow down whether they have managed to sneak in ten minutes of silence between their work day and their frantic shopping for the latest calming accessories. "Not yet," comes the good-natured reply from many during our first few sessions, "but I'm going to keep trying!"

Here's the reason to keep trying: when you learn to find that inner place of peace through self-reflection or meditation, you actually tune in to the perfect antidote — gentleness — to the most negative group energy you can find. Many of us are suffering from a gentleness

Learn to get in touch with the silence within yourself and know that everything in life has a purpose.

— Elisabeth Kübler-Ross

deficiency owing to the stressful demands of our day-to-day lives. This "energetic anemia" has become so advanced for some of us that we have forgotten what it feels like to feel good. Many people in our culture have become so accustomed to the rush they get from constant crises that they don't feel quite normal without a double espresso running through their system and a problem to focus on (don't worry, if there isn't one handy, they are easy to create). Meditation gives us a natural high that helps us put our problems into perspective while letting some natural energy light up the neurons for a change. By the way, there's a lovely side effect to learning to use natural energy as a pick-me-up rather than grabbing frantically for the nearest calorie or chemical boost: natural energy leaves us, well, happy.

Many people love the modern world's complexity, because it gives their well-trained, anxiously alert minds something to do. Thus, there is a humorous irony when the "experience junkies" come to the vital task of building a personal meditation practice. Meditation involves quieting the mind to key in to the innate simplicity of being. The irony is that some people search anxiously on the *outside* for books, gurus, and elaborate courses to help them "master" this concept.

Nothing in all creation is so like God as stillness.

— Meister Eckhart

For fast-acting relief, try slowing down.

— Lily Tomlin

EXERCISE:

DEVELOPING A PERSONAL MEDITATION PRACTICE

Find a time of day and a place you can habitually return to for your meditation practice. When you meditate and quiet your conscious mind, you are actually accessing a more primitive aspect of your consciousness that responds well to routine and rhythm. If you have experience dealing with animals and small children, you know how much they love the routine of being fed and held at a certain time. In a similar way, you soothe the savage beast in your own consciousness when you remember how powerfully aspects of your consciousness respond to regular stimulation.

It's far better to do ten minutes every day (okay, let's be reasonable for the type-A's out there — at least four days a week) than it is to do some fancy ritual in which you light incense, chant for hours, and astral project once a month! Like the Nike commercial says, "Just do it." This is why it helps to keep it simple. The investment of time is minimal, but the payoff is huge.

I encourage busy clients who are new to meditation to try this for *only* ten minutes a day in the beginning. Many habitual overachievers balk at this suggestion and come in grinning after a week telling me that they have been meditating for an hour a day. Inevitably they throw in the towel on the whole concept the following week. This is because if you demand too much from yourself in the beginning, you are likely to convince yourself that you don't have time to integrate this practice into your lifestyle.

Get an egg timer. Find a place that is quiet and comfortable and where you can be free from distractions. Set the timer for ten minutes. Close your eyes. Try one of the following while you sit there:

Patience is the companion of wisdom.

— Saint Augustine

- Count your breaths, counting from one to four over and over again. You can count on the inhale or on the exhale; you choose.

- Follow your stream of consciousness. Whatever thoughts you have, just acknowledge them and keep breathing. Thank any intrusive or anxious thoughts for bringing urgent information to your attention, acknowledge these thoughts, and let them pass.

- Focus on an internal symbol. This can be anything from the image of a candle to the memory of a peaceful place. Keep bringing your consciousness gently back to this symbol or image, and when distracting thoughts come in, acknowledge them, let them pass, and use your chosen mental image as an "anchor" or reference point that your consciousness can return to.

(Hint: You may want to keep a pad and pencil next to you for the first couple of weeks as you learn to meditate. If your mind presents you with an urgent "to do" list that makes it impossible to relax, simply open your eyes, write this list down, and start over.)

Janet came to coaching to develop a strategy for rebuilding her career as a travel agent after her firm had downsized. While Janet's husband was able to support them on his salary, she felt it was important to rebuild her career so that she and her husband could plan for their kids' college education and build a retirement fund together.

JANET

"I really want to be able to enjoy this time off and to make the most of this period in terms of self-reflection and personal growth. However, I'm so plagued by pervasive feelings of anxiety and self-doubt about my ability to rebuild my career that it's been difficult to relax and appreciate the fact that we still have enough money to survive. I've earned the right to enjoy that.

"Since I'm not working yet, I should have plenty of time to meditate. It's something I've wanted to learn to do for years, but I've never been able to stick with it. Frankly, while I was working, I was never able to fulfill any of the promises I made to myself. Everyone else's needs always came first.

"I was amazed by how hard it was to justify taking ten minutes to do this, even though I'm not working. I told myself the first night after we discussed this in coaching that I was going to get up before Dan and the kids and meditate while the house was quiet. Then I realized that I didn't want to set the alarm for fear of robbing Dan of the few precious minutes of extra sleep he deserves before heading for a job he's less than thrilled with. My solution? I'd meditate later in the day when the kids were at school.

"The first few days after our session seemed to take on a life of their own. Suddenly, there were tons of things that *had* to get done that all seemed like my top priority. One of our neighbor's kids was having a birthday party, so I decided to make cupcakes because his

Only when one is connected to one's own core is one connected to others. And, for me, the inner spring can best be found through solitude.

— Anne Morrow Lindbergh

mother has been so kind about helping me out with my sons while I was working. Then my mother-in-law kept me on the phone for over an hour hashing out plans for an upcoming family vacation. Another neighbor, whose husband recently passed away, needed me to pick up some groceries and some stuff at a hardware store for her. Hey, that last one was a *pleasure!* What's happened to their family is so tragic; I'd go to any lengths to help them out.

"However, when I looked back on my schedule and the fact that I hadn't found time to meditate for the first couple of days, I realized it wasn't because there was no time — *It was only ten little minutes* — it was because the prospect of slowing down internally to listen to myself was threatening as hell to me. I was afraid that if I slowed down, I might lose my momentum in the course of the day and not be able to start up again.

"When you first made this suggestion, I thought that ten minutes was too short a period to have any meaningful impact on my inner life. Now I realize that you suggested ten minutes because of how obviously ridiculous it is not to be able to fit this into one's schedule. I was forced to take a look at how I was prioritizing my time when I was caving on a tiny commitment to personal growth.

"By the third day, I forced myself to go for it. Those ten little minutes felt like an eternity! I actually had to open my eyes and peek at the egg timer because I was so anxious that it was broken and that I was wasting valuable time just sitting there — God forbid! My thoughts were all over the place. My mind kept anxiously dashing to the next thing on my 'to do' list. It was a good thing you told me to keep a pen and paper by my side while I did this for the first few weeks, and that it was okay to open my eyes and write down 'to dos' that occurred to me, as long as I rewound the timer and started over again. I had to do this a couple of times as I started this practice.

"One morning, I forced myself to breathe through my anxiety. All these thoughts about what I needed to get done started dive-bombing me, and as I tuned in to my body, I realized I was rigid with anxiety over

You must have a room or a certain hour of the day or so where you do not know what was in the morning paper . . . a place where you can simply experience and bring forth what you are, and what you might be. . . . At first you may find nothing's happening. . . . But if you have a sacred place and use it, take advantage of it, something will happen.

— Joseph Campbell

not doing enough. I practiced what you taught me about breathing into the area of physical tension and trying to accept what was there, and I realized that I felt tremendously guilty about not working. It was totally illogical, but somehow I felt it was my fault that my firm had offered me a package and let me go. Some totally irrational beliefs were kicking up in me, that if I had been smarter, or tougher, or wiser in some vague way I'd still have my job. Suddenly, I realized why I'd been rushing around so frantically. Since these feelings of guilt were irrational, I was devoting a great deal of internal energy to suppressing them.

"Another morning when I was meditating, I felt that familiar knot in my chest that kicks in when I'm feeling bad about losing my job and anxious that I'll never find another one. I remembered what you said about my conscious mind being hyperalert about potential problems because it was trying to protect me. I mentally thanked my mind for bringing to my attention, *yet again,* the fact that I was going to need a job in the future and continued to breathe. The knot in my chest started getting bigger. I just stayed detached and kept breathing. Ironically, the more that tight feeling in my chest grew, the more objective and amused my consciousness seemed to get. It was like a new voice inside of me was saying...this is the challenge...this is you...the two are not the same.

"Suddenly, without warning, I felt this 'pop,' or release, in my chest. I was flooded with a feeling of happiness and well-being that I was totally unprepared for. It was like psychic champagne. I felt wonderful, optimistic, and even giddy. I remembered what you had said about 'grounding energy' so, since I was sitting cross-legged in the kitchen, I put my hands on the floor on either side of me and counted my breaths until I was in touch with my body and felt solid.

"I went through the rest of the day with so much excess energy I barely knew what to do with myself. However, it was a kind of relaxed joyful energy — not the anxious adrenaline I usually use to whip myself into action. Since that experience, I've been hooked. I actually look forward to meditating, and I'm trying to energize myself more naturally by meditating rather than relying on constant infusions of

Relaxing makes me nervous.

— Unknown

caffeine and a laundry list of worries to keep me motivated. I haven't had another experience in meditation quite as dramatic as that first one, but I also remember your hint not to limit myself by trying to re-create a previous experience, that every time we meditate is unique.

"It's tough to put into words how much those simple ten minutes a day have enhanced the quality of my life. I'm more relaxed, more patient with my kids, and more optimistic about life in general. The benefits are subtle — but they are so all-encompassing that it's astounding."

There is no right way to meditate, and if your practice is working for you, please don't change it. When you are trying to release the grip of the demands of your "to do" list on your psyche long enough to connect with your inner world, the simpler the strategy, the better. If you allow your mind to overly complicate the concept of meditation, you will miss the point entirely and the role you play under pressure will be left to run things the way it sees fit — unhindered by the higher perspective of your authentic self.

Meditation is simple — as simple as breathing. Breath is both an important part of meditation and a great metaphor for it. We breathe involuntarily, though we can consciously regulate our breath when we choose to. Similarly, we are all constantly going in and out of various levels of consciousness. Some of these levels are more meditative than others. In developing a meditation practice, we are simply learning that when we focus on our level of consciousness we can learn to regulate it in a manner that is similar to the way that we can choose to control our breath at moments even though we breathe automatically.

Developing a consistent meditation practice has powerfully influenced my executive coaching over the years. When I began bringing my ideas about harmonizing people's intellectual, emotional, and spiritual focus into the workplace, I was immediately plunged into the

*Silence is a true friend
who never betrays.*

— Confucius

*Silence is the homeland
of the strong.*

— Tennyson

group energy of ambition, intrigue, and anxiety that permeates the very cultures that need this work the most.

Genius is eternal patience.

— Michelangelo

As I worked with clients who were fighting depression because they had been unable to find work or who were battling waves of paranoia because of the latest corporate turf war, I found that to bring a perspective of clarity into our work I had to find the time to meditate daily. When I didn't take the time to clear out my own emotional reactions and attachments to what my clients were experiencing, I could do little more than help them recycle the thoughts that were keeping them stuck.

We all possess many innate abilities and skills that, with only a slight shift in our conscious perspective of reality, we can remember how to use. In fact, these abilities are so simple and natural that it almost takes more effort to repress them than it does to use them. Think of how much energy it takes to rush around fast enough to distract yourself from your inner voice!

As you grow in your meditation practice, you will become more and more able to monitor the stream of conscious thoughts in your internal world. However, equally important is the ability to monitor the stream of chance meetings, opportunities, and events that take place in your external world, because these are manifestations of the way you have been focusing your energy.

This brings you to the next exercise in the Integration Stage. Now that you have considered bringing your authentic self to bear in becoming more aware of what's going on internally, it only makes sense to apply this expanded perspective of reality to include the external world as well.

EXERCISE:

YOUR SYNCHRONICITIES INVENTORY

One of the most basic and powerful psychological skills is the ability to focus your concentration. This is because what you pay attention to grows. In addition, your consciousness creates patterns that, if allowed to adapt to their environment, will eventually manifest in relationships, opportunities, and insights that can change your life.

One way you can train yourself to become aware of the impact that your consciousness has on your daily life is to notice the synchronicities or coincidences that are taking place around you all the time. Many people are addicted to anxiously controlling the events in their lives based on the reality of our mainstream culture. Noticing the way that people who come into our lives mirror aspects of ourselves that we need to be more aware of or the way that events unfold to bring us experiences that aid in our development is yet another way of being attuned to the authentic self. When you become aware of the synchronicities in your life, you begin to "uncreate" the blocks that keep you from trusting the way that your true self works. As you do this, you become less dependent on your concrete skills of controlling and manipulating people and situations, and you start to realize your professional dreams.

Swiss psychiatrist Carl Jung is credited with coining the term *synchronicities.* He used this word to describe meaningful coincidences that connect cause and effect. Jung noted, "Synchronicity suggests there is an interconnection or unity of causally unrelated events." The belief in the power of synchronicities has become widespread. People who embrace their spirituality frequently quote the slogan "there are no accidents." Students of Eastern philosophy are familiar with the ideology that "we create our own luck." Students of metaphysics are encouraged to keep dream diaries so that they can record ways in which they may "remember the future" as well as the past in less restricted moments of consciousness. For anyone who hopes to create a vital career in an uncertain employment market, this more open role that our authentic self plays in speaking to us through the people and events that surround us in our daily lives can be very powerful. From one perspective, industries are contracting and the economic landscape can seem hopelessly bleak. From the perspective of the authentic self, every challenge carries

To know the truth, one must get rid of knowledge. Nothing is more powerful and creative than emptiness.

— Lao-tzu

within it the seed of an opportunity. For example, I have had clients come to me stunned by the abruptness with which they had been fired from jobs they were hanging on to simply to pay the bills. Fueled by financial fears, many of them have taken career risks such as interviewing in new industries or starting businesses that they might have considered a frivolous risk of their job 'security' if being downsized hadn't left them with nothing to lose. Often, these clients will report that chance meetings on an airplane or even while standing in line buying a cup of coffee have led to career breaks and helped them to defy the odds by breaking into a new industry in a tough economy. One client, laid off from her job with a big publisher, finally started a freelance editing business — something she'd dreamed of for years — after having one meaningful conversation with a stranger.

Set aside an hour of quiet time to answer the following questions:

I will teach you the best way to say Torah. You must be nothing but an ear that hears what the universe of the word is constantly saying within you. The moment you begin to hear what you yourself are saying, you must stop.

— Dov Baer of Mezritch

1. Can you identify a coincidence that has had a meaningful impact on your life?

2. Have you met anyone recently who mirrors back to you your greatest vulnerabilities? How did she or he come into your life?

3. Who mirrors the personality traits that you value in yourself? How did this individual come into your life?

4. What series of relationships and events led to your current or last job opportunity? Were there any important coincidences involved?

5. What is the most important relationship in your life today? What dreams or desires were prominent in your consciousness before you met this person?

6. Do you remember any dreams about significant people or events in your life that later proved to be important in terms of life events that took place? If so, what were these?

John, an options trader at a securities firm, had come for coaching because, although he felt his job was secure, he had lost his sense of purpose and his enthusiasm for his work.

JOHN

"Everything I do is very transactions oriented," John told me. "I simply can't get excited about picking up the phone and trying to get clients interested in putting on trades anymore. My firm has gotten so big that I no longer feel like I'm part of anything meaningful. I just feel like a cog in a big machine. I'm on contract, so my job is secure right now, but I feel so bored and useless that it's really getting to me.

"Doing this exercise gave me a great deal of hope. It would be easy for me to slip into despair right now. My feelings might seem self-centered, because I can afford to support my family, and I know plenty of people who are struggling right now, but I still need to work to put aside enough savings to get four kids through college — and the cost of raising a family just seems to go up every day.

"Before I came for coaching, I'd had a variety of conversations with my accountant and my lawyer about how I could network with people to find a position I could get excited about again. Frankly, it just felt hopeless to me because the job market has been so tight.

"The first question in this exercise caused me to remember the frustration I felt about my career in the late 1980s. At that time, I was a struggling trading assistant looking for a chance to take on more responsibility on any trading floor that would have me. I was also in my first year of recovery and was going to AA regularly. This helped me deal with the fear of never making it in my career as much as it helped me stay out of bars.

"I remember doing a lot of praying in those years, and one afternoon I read about a big investment conference featuring some of the top traders. My boss frowned on our going to those sorts of things, but something in my gut told me this was one I didn't want to miss. When I couldn't get my boss to approve my attendance at the conference, I actually took a sick day and paid the entrance fee out of my own pocket.

To do great work, man must be very idle as well as very industrious.

Samuel Butler

"The morning of the event, I was sick as a dog. I'd gotten a cold, I was running a fever, and I was toying with the idea of forgetting the whole thing. However, I kept going back to the brochure indicating that a top trader I'd been reading about in the *Wall Street Journal* was actually going to speak. I felt like I had to try and meet this guy for some reason — so I downed some cold medicine and forced myself to go.

"The conference was jammed, and the session where this guy was speaking was particularly mobbed. I somehow managed to get a seat in front, and I decided to give it my best shot. The panel discussion got me really excited. However, all the guys on the panel came in with assistants who looked like their job was to get them in and out as quickly as possible.

"When the presentation was over, I went up to Jason, the trader I had hoped to meet. I was stuck in a group of eight people who were trying to get his attention. I made eye contact with him, and he knew I was waiting. By the time I got a chance to speak to him, he was on his way out the door. I handed Jason my business card, and words I never expected to utter just started flooding out of me. I told him how much I wanted to be a trader and all the things I was doing to learn my craft. I asked him if he would possibly be willing to let me take him to lunch to get some pointers on how I could position myself. Jason paused, looked me up and down, and then handed me his business card and told me to tell his secretary to put me on his calendar. I was so excited and relieved — not to mention sick — that I thought I was going to faint.

"Two weeks later, Jason and I met for lunch. He told me about how he had started his career, and there were some similarities between us that surprised us both. He suggested that I send him three copies of my résumé, and he would take it from there.

"Jason called up the heads of trading of three of the most prominent Wall Street firms and got me interviews with all three of them. I had landed my first job as a trader in under a month.

"I tried to keep in touch with Jason, but he eventually left the business and retired a wealthy man. The few times we did come in

To hear the voice of the voiceless, we must be silent.

— Unknown

contact with each other, he mentioned that he didn't know exactly what it was about me that had inspired him to help me out, but that he was glad that he had.

"Six years later, I was a successful trader, and my beautiful wife was pregnant with our second child. I decided to go back to the first AA meeting I had attended when I first began my recovery to celebrate the anniversary of my sobriety and my gratitude about how well my life was going. It turned out to be a meeting where people who had long-term sobriety were sharing their personal stories for other members of the group. Guess who was up at the podium celebrating fourteen years of sobriety? Jason! We spotted each other across the room, and I think we both got chills. He had no idea I was in recovery, and I had no idea that he was, but somehow I was guided to meet him, and he was guided to help me.

"As I completed the other questions in this exercise, I realized that more than a few other coincidences were operating in my life. Completing this gave me a surge of hope. I realized that, even when things look grim from a concrete perspective, my true self is ready and willing to go to bat for me if I can trust myself enough to get out of the way and let it happen."

We are sick with a fascination for the useful tools of names and numbers, of symbols, signs, conceptions and ideas. Meditation is therefore the art of suspended verbal and symbolic thinking for a time, somewhat as a courteous audience will stop talking when a concert is about to begin.

— **Alan Watts**

Becoming attuned to synchronicities is about cultivating a new way of listening to your authentic self. Life is an energetic web of interconnected possibilities. Our real self speaks to us through the people and events that come to us in the course of a day. We shut down this channel of communication when we become so anxious that we are unable to trust our authentic self and when we become too narrowly focused on controlling specific events rather than going with the flow.

Some additional ways to strengthen your awareness of the synchronicities in your life is to discuss important coincidences with

trusted members of your support group. The energy that creates fortu-
itous events is amplified when you focus on it, and it is further
amplified when you validate the truth of these events and the way they
are supporting your growth by discussing them with others.

You may also want to keep a journal by your bed to record any
dreams or flashes of insight that occur to you when your consciousness
is less restricted. The authentic self responds favorably when it is validated and appreciated. Acknowledge the contribution that your true
self is making to your professional evolution in unofficial as well as
official ways, and those coincidences will multiply.

*If the mind can get quiet
enough, something sacred
will be revealed.*

— Helen Tworkov

Defining success is one of our major challenges today. Our definition of success has been polluted by the nonstop images of conspicuous consumption that the media promotes as the American Dream. Teeth are grinding in the middle of the night across the nation as the internal war between "having it all" and a sense of commitment to the financial security of employees (and shareholders) rages in the subconscious of many executives.

As you strengthen your ability to trust yourself more fully and to evolve into a more successful professional, you may find that the way that you measure success evolves as well. Often people who begin this work to gain financial security and personal influence gradually find that they become much more interested in contributing to their organizations and their communities at a deeper level. People who have contributed erratically to charitable and civic causes because they felt too powerless or exhausted to believe they could make a difference gradually have evolved into individuals who realize that they have the power and influence to make a difference in areas they care about.

As you integrate your beliefs about personal gain and your beliefs about your responsibility, you will find that you automatically unite the drives elicited by these powerful desires and operate by a definition of success that is not sabotaged by internal conflict. This holistic approach to career development not only maximizes your chances of success, it also ensures that this success will be defined authentically.

As discussed previously, our beliefs are thoughts that have been saturated with our expectations and emotions. It is through our beliefs — those ideas about reality that are backed by the emotional fuel either of desire or dread — that our authentic self is able to translate the terrain of our inner world into the physical reality of our life. Often beliefs hide from our conscious awareness by disguising themselves as "facts."

CHAPTER 12

Maintaining an Interdependent Perspective

It's vital that we remain mindful of the distinction between beliefs and facts, because many of these so-called facts limit us from achieving our true potential.

The man who dies rich . . . dies disgraced.
— Andrew Carnegie

"I'm too sensitive to be successful in a competitive environment . . . I'm too shy to stand in front of a classroom . . . I'm not smart enough to learn to use a computer this late in life . . . I'm too poor to take the risk of starting my own business" are all examples of the kind of beliefs that can masquerade as facts if we don't remain vigilant about questioning the ideas that stand between our current reality and our true potential.

The following exercise is about being mindful of your beliefs so that you can create the success of your dreams and avoid staying stuck in the rut of your nightmares.

EXERCISE:

EXPANDING YOUR DEFINITION OF SUCCESS

This five-part exercise goes full circle to draw on many of the insights you developed doing the first exercise in the book, the Personal Tree of Life. You will want to review the work you did in the Awareness Stage as you answer the questions in this exercise.

Begin by taking a few minutes to write down your current definition of success in your journal. Then answer the following questions:

1. How does my definition of success affect me?
2. How does my definition of success influence the way that others react to me?
3. Do I appear successful to myself? Why or why not?
4. Do I appear successful to others? Why or why not?

Now consider your feelings about success depending on how you answer the following questions:

1. How does your current age affect your potential for success?
2. How does your gender affect your potential for success?

3. How does your physical appearance and/or physical health affect your potential for success?
4. How does your ethnic background, sexual orientation, or religious preference affect your potential for success?
5. How does your marital status affect your potential for success?
6. How does your level of education affect your potential for success?
7. How does your previous job experience affect your potential for success?

Now make a list in your journal of all the people who are significant to you at this time. This list should include your professional peers, your friends, and members of your family who you speak with or think about regularly. It may also include prominent political figures or even media celebrities who have strongly shaped your thoughts and feelings about success. As you answer the following questions, bear in mind that we are drawn to the significant people in our life (particularly those we have strong negative reactions to) based on the inner similarities in our belief systems. For example, many clients who complain about their boss's short attention span and lack of availability realize, upon reflection, that their own tendency to overschedule themselves and rush through their days amplifies their frustration when they notice this tendency in others. Considering these significant individuals one at a time, reflect on the following questions:

Life is too beautiful, how shall I bear it? Love answered musingly, why don't you share it?

—Unknown

1. How do I think this individual would define success?
2. Does this person consider her- or himself successful? Why or why not?
3. How important a role does this person play in my life?
4. How are my beliefs about success similar to this person's? How do they differ?
5. Are the beliefs about success that I share with this person reflective of my role or of my authentic self?
6. If I were operating more consistently from my authentic self, how would my beliefs about success influence my relationship with this person?

In this part of the exercise, bear in mind that many of your intellectual assumptions about success are based on what you think you "should" believe, while your emotional reactions to these concepts are often more reflective of your true beliefs.

1. How do you feel when you reflect on the beliefs about success that are fostered in your workplace?

2. How do you feel when you reflect on the beliefs about success that are prominent in your family?

3. Which of your beliefs about success do you "feel" to be true — even though you know better logically?

4. What beliefs do you hold because you think that they make you a "good person"? (Warning: The toughest limiting beliefs to spot are those you believe to be "good.")

5. What other thoughts are behind these beliefs?

6. How do you feel when you reflect on your life in light of your current definition of success?

Finally, by answering the following questions, evaluate your current beliefs about success:

1. What aspects of your current thoughts and feelings about success are limiting your authentic potential?

2. What aspects of your current thoughts and feelings are supporting your authentic potential?

3. How can you expose yourself to more ideas, relationships, and situations that nurture your authentic potential?

Even if you are able to answer the questions in one evening, put your answers aside and review them a few days later to see how your evolving definition of success continues to resonate with you.

Candice, a single working mother and a portfolio manager, was experiencing what she admitted was a "high-class" problem as she tackled this exercise. Candice had struggled for years after divorcing her first husband to maintain her fund's performance and be a single parent.

No person was ever honored for what he received. Honor has been the reward for what he gave.

— Calvin Coolidge

She had recently fallen in love and gotten engaged, and she was now contemplating how to reconcile her commitment to her investors with her desire to have a second child and commit more fully to building the family she had always dreamed of.

CANDICE

"As I went back to the beginning of this process and reviewed my work from the Personal Tree of Life exercise, it was clear to me that most of my ideas about success have mirrored those of my father. My dad was a tenured professor at an Ivy League college, and, as far back as I can remember, my sense of self has been defined by my being at the top of my class.

"Getting ahead in a corporate environment was much harder for me than getting ahead in school, because socializing was always awkward for me. Since I'd always defined success in terms of intellectual accomplishments, I was a slow learner when it came to things like networking and business socializing. However, once I figured out that I was going to have to develop personal relationships with my colleagues to get ahead, I worked hard at it.

"While I always craved a female mentor, the healthiest relationships I was able to form were with men. I'd felt particularly distrustful of women after working under a female boss who pretended to support other women to get attention from senior management, while she subtly refused to lift a finger to further the careers of the women reporting to her.

"As I answered the questions in this exercise, I was forced to reexamine several core beliefs about success that had been creating conflict within me for some time. First, I realized that I was dealing with a belief that success should be related to hard work and intelligence. While this belief came from my dad, it was definitely not reinforced by my experience in

You can never do
a kindness too soon,
for you never know how
soon it will be too late.

— Ralph Waldo Emerson

my work environment. Year after year on the job, I kept seeing promotions go to young men who came in and managed to suceed with ease at the expense of hard-working women with more tenure in their departments. Basically, I experienced a tremendous amount of resentment when life was not 'fair' according to the rules I had been raised with.

"This discouraging situation fed another dark and powerful belief that men were simply the natural leaders in society and that the place for a woman was at home, raising a family and keeping her mouth shut. The problem there was, as a woman who had graduated from Harvard with a degree in applied mathematics, I'd developed a need for intellectual stimulation that was as much a part of my being as my need for oxygen.

"Finally, this exercise made me realize that I was experiencing some conflict between my ideas about what it meant to be successful as a professional and what it meant to be successful as a woman. As a professional, the definition for success as corporate America defined it was pretty straightforward. You amassed as much power and money as you could — period. As a woman, however, things are more complex. I knew at some deep level of my being that I never wanted to sacrifice my femininity. However, femininity is complicated to define, particularly in a corporate context. Most of the women with whom I discussed the concept of 'corporate femininity' described it as the need for creative expression, respectful treatment from others, and an overall sense of satisfaction with their careers that involved their professional relationships as well as their accomplishments. I came to believe that a 'feminine' definition of success encompassed a whole list of experiential and emotional perks that a more male definition of success didn't include.

"As I considered the ways many of the significant people in my life would define success, I realized that there were some rampant contradictions in how they dealt with the concept. Most of my male colleagues defined success as having the power and money to do what they wanted with their lives and provide for their families in the process. Many of my female friends from business school, who are feeling

We cannot know whether or not we love God . . . but we can know whether or not we love our neighbor. And be certain that the more advanced you see you are in love for your neighbor the more advanced you will be in the love of God.

— Teresa of Avila

burned out by the demands of their jobs and are anxious about their biological clocks, feel that success involves not only being great at their work but also being able to manage their jobs in a way that leaves them free to raise families as well. Then there's my mom, who simply defines success as being able to raise a healthy family in a loving way.

"There was a definite split in my definition of success. Not only was I longing for the ability to achieve individual recognition for my professional abilities, but I was also plagued by recurrent waves of self-doubt over whether or not I was successful in using my feminine ability to nurture the relationships around me. I realized that much of my energy was drained by this internal battle between competing concepts of success that took place when, no matter what I'd achieved professionally, I kept wondering if I was a good-enough daughter, a good-enough mentor to other women . . . hell, I spent nights wondering if I was a good-enough date!

"As I launched into the feelings part of this exercise, I began to understand how the war raging inside me between these competing concepts left me angry and exhausted much of the time. It was as if I couldn't win. If I was successful as a professional, then I wasn't a good-enough mother. The resentful looks I get from the mothers who don't work when I come rushing into parent events late at my daughter's school have sent me into a frenzy of suppressed resentment and self-loathing. Meanwhile, I have to deal with my own feelings of rage when one of my female colleagues gets free time and support for her maternity leave, while I had to come back to work within weeks of having my daughter because I was afraid of losing my job. What's more, I had to cut our honeymoon short because a few expectant mothers in our department might be giving birth at around the same time we were planning to have our wedding. Some days I felt like a monster being angry at my female colleagues who needed some slack so they could 'have it all.' But it just didn't seem fair that I'd had to struggle so hard with my own pregnancy and now I had to make even more personal sacrifices to give them the help I'd never gotten.

The earth does not belong to us, we belong to it.

— Black Elk

What is a true gift?
One for which nothing is
expected in return.

— Confucius

"As I tuned in to the thoughts behind the beliefs, I realized that one of the other emotionally charged thoughts that was keeping me stuck was the conviction that I was in this all alone and that nobody was going to help me. My ex-husband had never been much help. Whenever I got frustrated he just stormed out of the room and accused me of being too sensitive. What's more, the woman I had worked for when I was pregnant managed to negotiate a generous maternal leave for herself and then turned around and threatened to fire any woman working for her who even considered asking for similar consideration. Senior management, of course, thought this woman was a staunch supporter of other women and was completely unaware of this dynamic.

"I kept coming back to your reminder that beliefs can masquerade as facts, and that I needed to test some of my most basic assumptions to see if things were really as dire as I was convincing myself they were. To test my assumption that 'nobody cared about me' I asked my new male manager and the woman who was in charge of running our internal diversity program to have lunch with me to discuss my situation.

"I explained the powerful mixed feelings I was experiencing based on my circumstances when I had my first child. I also alluded to the resentment I felt about how the firm's current diversity programs seemed to gloss over the complexities about how women, who often had powerfully different reactions to the work-life balance issue, related to each other. As I did this, I managed to stay emotionally connected with my boss and the head of our diversity program and to deliver my concerns without any emotional edge.

"I was amazed at the feedback they gave me. First, my boss, Dave, thanked me for helping him consider an interpersonal aspect of the work-balance issue that he hadn't considered before. He assured me that he would personally make sure that I got the time I needed to have the honeymoon I deserved, and that if I was still working for him when I got pregnant again, he would make sure that I got as much consideration as any other women in the firm with my maternity leave. Second, the head of our diversity task force told me that she had recently read the exit interviews of a few women who had worked for my old boss and that she had long suspected that there was a double standard during this period but had been unable to prove it. Sharon asked me to volunteer to be a speaker at the next diversity workshop to help give talented women in our firm permission to discuss the complex issues of work-life balance so that the firm could support us more effectively.

"I reflected on this meeting as I did the final part of this exercise on defining success. I realized that it was important for me to test my limiting beliefs whenever possible. I also realized that I was one of many people, men as well as women, tackling the hard work of defining success in an era when everyone's definition was taking on a more balanced aspect. Once I realized this, I was able to share my perspective in the spirit of helping others in the organization. This work is helping me understand that working through my limiting beliefs is the key to achieving a definition of success that doesn't require unwholesome compromises — either personally or professionally."

Never doubt that a small group of thoughtful, committed people can change the world. Indeed, it is the only thing that ever can.

— Margaret Mead

We are all connected through our longing for a sense of purpose and creative expression. I realized the importance of this concept years ago when I was one of two portfolio managers working with a group of talented bond and currency traders in Boston.

In those days, it was common for us to travel internationally to get a deeper sense of what was going on in the domestic economies of the countries issuing the international government bonds we were holding in our portfolios. It was also common for our bond traders to make at least one trip a year to meet their counterparts in these countries with whom they spoke over the phone.

One of our bond traders was a talented young woman who specialized in covering the markets in Australia and New Zealand. She came into my office late one evening (this woman was regularly on the desk until 8:00 or 8:30 P.M.) and asked if she might schedule a business trip to New Zealand to visit the traders overseas whom she dealt with daily. I thought this was more than reasonable and told her all she had to do was get approval from the other lead portfolio manager in our group and it was a done deal.

You are what you share.

— Neal Walsh

Twenty minutes later, she was back in my office door — her eyes filled with tears this time. "I hate him!" she spat venomously. "He turned me down flat. He says we are spending too much on travel this year. He gets to travel lots more than he needs to. Hell, he goes to Tokyo just to practice his Japanese! I hate this place!"

I was devastated to see such a talented young woman so demoralized. This was not a woman who cried easily (frankly, I'd worked with her for four years and I'd never seen her that worked up), so obviously she was feeling exhausted and unappreciated by the way her request was received. My main concern at that point was that money couldn't buy the dedication with which this young lady kept an eagle eye on our Asian fixed income positions. For the price of a lousy coach ticket to New Zealand, we'd let one of the integral members of the team storm home that night feeling like she didn't give a damn.

Minutes later, the colleague who had inspired this resentful tirade was at my door looking a bit worked up himself. "You wouldn't believe what she wanted from us," he began defensively. After he'd made his position more than clear, my ears were ringing with his self-centered summation, "I mean, she gets a few good meals out of this job and a decent salary...what the hell does she want?"

Welcome to a no-win situation.

I was praying to keep the sarcasm and outrage out of my voice as I replied quietly, "Oh, I don't know...is it possible she wants the same things you and I want? To develop the kind of insight on international events you can only cultivate by seeing the world? To know she matters to us and to the firm? Maybe she defines success the same way we do." While I tried to sound like I was just brainstorming philosophically, I knew that my position was pretty transparent on this one and that taking a stand with him was risky.

Actually, this guy wasn't a bad person. He was just someone who measured success in terms of his personal, immediate gain and didn't see the connection between our team's morale and our bottom-line profitability.

Upon reflection, I owe them both a debt of tremendous gratitude because that evening was one of many moments that helped me understand that great leaders are the ones who make everyone on his or her team believe that the success of the department is due to their individual efforts.

At each stage of our growth, something new breaks forth. Our definition of success will evolve as we progress through the major turning points of our life. Paradoxically, getting in touch with our authentic sense of self and understanding our reactions to the challenges around us at a deeper level are what make it possible for us to wake up to the reality that we are not alone in our pursuit of success and that the people around us matter.

The more outwardly we see things, the more we define success from an individual rather than from a collective perspective. In contrast, the inner journey of getting in touch with our true selves begins individually but leads us to a communal perspective because it is our most personal desires in life that link us most powerfully to what we have in common with others. Thus, the more your definition of success is driven by the perspective of your authentic self, the more it will naturally orient you to the welfare of others.

It's only when we truly know and understand that we have a limited time on earth — and that we have no way of knowing when our time is up — that we will begin to love each day to the fullest, as if it was the only one we had.

— Elisabeth Kübler-Ross

EXERCISE:

A LETTER TO YOUR FUTURE SELF

In this final exercise you will be using the power of your authentic self to reach out to your future self both emotionally and imaginatively in order to get things flowing in the direction of your genuine desires.

Now, this idea of shifting our inner emotional currents by reaching out to the future self sounds pretty fantastic to many people. This is because in this culture most of us have been taught to think of time as linear and sequential. This linear definition of time leads most of us to be rather backward-looking in our self-definition. We define ourselves by the sum total of the experiences and interactions with others that we can remember from the past.

However, the emotions and desires that emanate from our being at any moment in time influence the patterns that create our future. Thus, if we remain addictively bonded to the thought patterns and emotional currents that have characterized our past, we will keep creating situations that give us the opportunity to recycle the same dramas in life over and over again. However, by connecting with the perspective of the authentic self, we are able to envision a wider range of possibilities and to shift these energetic patterns to create new opportunities for ourselves personally and professionally.

In this exercise you will write a letter to your future self. You will need paper and a pen and an uninterrupted block of time. As you write this letter to your future self, be sure to stay in touch with your breath and the sensations in your body that may come up. You may want to mention specific ways that you plan to cultivate your ability to access your inner wisdom to help you grow authentically. For many people, doing this exercise presents an opportunity to consider various types of creative expression, community involvement, or even spiritual study as they take the next step in the Authentic Career Process.

In writing this letter it is often most helpful to focus on the fact that this amazing authentic self you have tapped is most likely still appearing to you in its infancy. Bear in mind that we tend to tap in to the energy of the authentic self at the chronological age we reached when our true selves went into hibernation. The point of this letter is to allow you to access a sense of your future potential as you mature in your ability to operate from authenticity. You see, when you actually get involved below the neck, all sorts of amazing things start happening. A

Where there is great love there are always miracles.

—Willa Cather

tremendous amount of energetic power is just patiently "hanging out" in our bodies waiting to see if we ever get bored enough with TV reruns and idle snacking to tap into it.

When you are done writing the letter, take another short break.

After this break, take some time to write in your journal or laptop about how you felt writing this letter. Put your letter in a self-addressed stamped envelope and mail it to yourself at home. This allows some incubation time for the emotions you have unlocked by doing this exercise. When your letter arrives, open it and put it somewhere where you can see it daily.

Stanley, whom we met way back in the first exercise in this book, had come a long way by the time he reached this final exercise in the Authentic Career Process. Doing the Letter to Your Future Self exercise helped Stanley integrate the introspective and interactive work he had done throughout his coaching process into an ongoing commitment to his success.

STANLEY

"This exercise was much easier for me in terms of my personal life than it was in terms of my career," Stanley told me. "My authentic self was raring to go in using many of the talents that had been dormant for years as I had been slavishly focused on my work. Before settling down to do this exercise, I collected some old pictures of myself when I'd played with a rock band in college. I took these up into the study with me and started brainstorming about how I was going to get in touch with a group of guys and get a band going again.

"However, when I tried to contemplate how I was going to function differently at work, I got stuck," he admitted. "You see, when it comes to the work situation, my job isn't all that bad. I realized that I

I think that education is power. I think that being able to communicate is power. One of my main goals on the planet is to encourage people to empower themselves.

— Oprah Winfrey

don't want to quit my job, but I sure want to do it differently. The problem is that most of my challenges aren't even related to the market being down. They are due to *me* being down because the politics are so competitive. None of us really work as a team anymore, because we are all concerned that if we don't look like we are doing better than the guys sitting next to us we are going to be the next heads to roll.

"One thing I've learned, in many different ways, by going through this process is that when I'm being true to myself I find it much easier to trust others, or at least to give them the benefit of the doubt, than I do when I'm playing my role. As a result, when I'm coming from the perspective of my authentic self, it's easier to believe that my future will work out favorably.

"As I had this moment of optimism, I had my first conscious experience of asking my authentic self a direct question. 'Do you mean that this concept of being true to myself applies in all situations, even when *money* is on the line?' I found myself asking myself in shock. I mean, practical spirituality is fine in a meditation session, but carrying this concept over to the realm of cold, hard cash seemed just a bit fanatic. I could hardly believe it when my authentic self actually answered me! I'm still not sure if I actually heard a voice or just 'knew' when this thought popped into my head, but this idea was not generated by the frenzied mental confusion I was working with in forming the question, that's for sure. This serene, clear voice in my mind simply said, 'Yes . . . always trust your inner knowing.' At that moment, in my mind's eye I saw a blue glass cube getting shattered by a mallet. I'm still not sure what this meant symbolically, but what I do know is I felt the most tremendous emotional release. Suddenly, I was much clearer about what I wanted to do in my work situation, and the rest of the exercise flowed.

"I found myself writing to my future self that I wanted to have successfully surmounted the interpersonal challenges in my firm so that I could be considered a leader in the field based on my commitment to hard work and my fairness to my colleagues. I wrote that, even if I got laid off from my current job, I was going to work so hard that other firms would be clamoring to have me. I realized that I'd been so

There is hope if people will begin to awaken that spiritual part of themselves — that heartfelt acknowledgement that we are the caretakers of life on this planet.

— Black Elk

focused on getting a great deal for myself that I hadn't really focused on doing a great job for my firm. I decided that I was going to *truthfully* work hard at this job and trust that the universe would take care of me if I did this. My authentic self realized that most of the people I was working with were giving far less than their top effort in their work because they were so disheartened and confused about what they wanted.

"To continue nurturing my mind-body connection, I decided to register for a meditation course. I never thought I'd consider doing this to further my professional advancement — frankly, I never thought I was the kind of guy who'd consider doing this at all — but the work I've done throughout this process has helped me understand that there is a practical link between my connection with myself and my ability to achieve my long-term career goals.

"I also realized that I was going to take the time for myself and my family. I was going to be the best, but part of that meant I was going to stand up to the group energy around me when it was crazy. I realized that I was working both for my family's well-being and for my firm and that I had the power and the presence to balance both these goals in a healthy way. Trust and truth — what a concept!

"If anyone had suggested this plan to me a few months ago, I would have dismissed them and assumed that operating on such principles would brand me as a sap. Let me tell you, this has been a stressful year professionally! However, as I continued to reflect on this exercise, I realized that there was tremendous power in trusting myself — and that this power could create anything. Of course, to do this I have to operate from integrity and truth because now I don't know any other way to play."

You are not a Muslim if there is one person in your neighborhood who goes to sleep hungry.

— Muhammad

It's important to keep this letter where you can see it daily to reinforce your commitment to your ongoing growth and to remind you of the hard work you have done in committing to a deeper level of personal insight, emotional courage, interpersonal effectiveness, and authentic success.

This exercise draws from one of the most challenging aspects of my own experience. I was helped through this experience by spontaneously writing a letter *from* my future self. This exercise eventually evolved into the one you just completed, where you write a letter *to* your future self. One year during my portfolio management career in Boston was particularly dark for me emotionally. Senior management was struggling with the decision of whether or not to sell our privately owned investment firm, the savings and loan crisis was threatening the integrity of the capital markets, and my love life was on the rocks — again. I was crawling home from work every night exhausted and discouraged, and I was having such trouble getting out of bed in the morning that I was terrified I was losing the precious energy I needed to keep functioning.

My weekly therapy sessions weren't cutting it. I felt like I was simply rehashing the same litany of complaints over and over — and I wasn't feeling any better. I was becoming socially isolated, and I'd pretty much lost interest in dating altogether. The worst part of this period was, even when I prayed, I felt cut off from a disinterested Higher Power who couldn't be bothered with my whining.

In the deepest recesses of my being, I knew that I had what it took to pull myself out of this dark night of the soul if only I could find the key to unlock my inner strength. I longed to find a helping professional, a spiritual leader, or even a friend who could tell me what I so desperately needed to hear to keep going, but my outer world seemed as much of an inspirational desert as my inner one.

One night, I was so desperate that I did something really crazy. I decided to imagine that I had already survived this insanely discouraging period of my life and finally had become the woman I wished I could be. With a trembling hand, I wrote a letter to the tired, confused, and lonely woman I was that night from the woman in the

We find in life exactly what we put into it.

— Ralph Waldo Emerson

future who had survived these challenges and lived to take on new ones. I reminded this tired woman that the idea that she was completely alone in the world was a distortion. I reminded her that love, fulfillment, and self-respect were possible, even in what often felt like an insensitive and uncaring world. I reminded her that the spiritual dimension was real. I also reminded her that if she couldn't find someone to help her work through her challenges, then she needed to become that person herself.

The next morning, the grind of routine stuffed me neatly back into my performance-oriented rut. I was obediently trudging to the office before the sun came up, fueled by enough coffee to wake a baby elephant. What's more, for the next couple of days, the low-grade depression that had become my emotional equilibrium left me with just enough energy to keep cranking out trades and "doing the drill" at work with robotic precision.

A few days later, armed with a small bag of groceries and an overflowing briefcase, I was perfunctorily opening my mailbox and dreading the armload of junk mail I would have to juggle until I could get to my trash can. On the top of my mail pile was a letter that I had addressed to myself. I had forgotten that in my altered state of desperation and insanity a couple of nights before, I had actually gone all the way over the edge and addressed the letter from my future self to my present self and *mailed* the darned thing around midnight. I winced when I first saw it — I had wasted a stamp in a moment of fantasy. Maybe I should have a chat with my therapist about some kind of medication. Surely I was losing it.

However, when I got to my kitchen and began purposefully dumping credit card applications and catalogs into the trash, I couldn't pitch this letter. It sat there on my kitchen counter as my own address, written in my own scrawled handwriting, stared back at me. After a few moments, I decided "what the hell, I'm nuts anyway" and decided to read the letter before turning on the evening news.

I sat down in my living room with a cup of coffee and ripped it

To be compassionate is to wish that a being or all beings be free from pain. To be compassionate is to sense from within what it must be like to experience someone else's experience.

— Sharon Salzberg

Why aren't you happy?
It's because ninety-nine
percent of everything
you do, and think,
and say is for yourself.

— Wu Wei Wu

open. Good thing I was sitting down — because the emotions that swept over me when I read this letter again left me sobbing.

It seems there was some aspect of my consciousness that had opened up when I wrote this letter that had found the exact words I needed to find the strength to keep going. This wasn't just a letter — it was a prayer. It was a prayer I had sent out to whatever God I could conceive of in the desperation to find the strength I needed to keep going. However, as I read that letter in my living room, I realized that now this was my Higher Power's prayer back to me.

During the following months, I kept praying in this way. The amazing part of this "U.S. postal ritual" was that it taught me that the most important part of writing is not just the writing itself (which, by the way, is an amazing meditation) but rather that reading what we have written helps us build a friendship with ourselves that is the foundation of true self-esteem.

When you receive your letter to your future self in the mail, you've graduated. Think of this letter as your diploma and your mission statement all rolled into one. It's vital to remember that completing this process is not an ending. This process is intended to help you build a solid foundation for the next step of your personal and professional development. Many wonderful resources are available that you can use as a next step in your ongoing growth. Hopefully the Authentic Career Process has helped you to understand the natural sequence of the way that we take in new ideas mentally (the Awareness Stage), process them emotionally (the Emotional Ownership Stage), make them our own by acting on them with others (the Interaction Stage), and, finally, assimilate them into our constantly evolving sense of self (the Integration Stage). Know that you can apply the principles of this process to give you a framework for working with any new body of knowledge — be this a new industry you are learning or a new spiritual philosophy you are exploring — so that you are able to work with these new concepts at all levels of your being.

Many of the clients who graduate from my practice take part in a special termination ritual. I ask each client who completes this process to write a few words about what he or she considers most valuable in the course of the work and what his or her dreams and plans are for the future. I have a large book that was designed for me by an artist I worked with, and each graduating client has the opportunity to take this book home for a few days to read the anonymous comments of previous clients while they script their words of wisdom for the clients that will come after them. It can be quite powerful for clients who have done this work to read the insights of people who have gone through this process to help them launch careers in everything from restaurant management to the creative arts.

My inspiration for this particular termination ritual came from my growing understanding that, in many ways, a book is a sacred metaphor for a human being. I've always loved books, ever since I was a child. Just as a book is filled with words, symbols, and pictures, so is a human consciousness filled with words, symbols, and pictures that carry a unique charge. Just as "you can't judge a book by its cover," so it is dangerous to judge a human being merely by the way he or she dresses or the role he or she plays to the outside world. Most important, just as no two human beings will have the same experience reading the same book, every time two human beings interact, a unique energy is created between them.

Some people have told me they have formed groups to work through the Authentic Career Process together. If you have done this work in conjunction with members of your support group, you may want to create a book for the group that includes everyone's insights on the process. This way you can have a permanent record of what you have shared working together. Rereading such a book during future challenges can give you the energy you need to keep focused on your authentic dreams.

Be prepared at all times for the gifts of God and be ready for new ones. For God is a thousand times more ready to give than we are to receive.

— **Meister Eckhart**

Conclusion

Now that you have completed the Authentic Career Process, please remember that this is not an ending, it is a beginning. Deepening your relationship with your authentic self, the foundation of your ability to be successful without sacrificing your personal power, is a never-ending process. The Authentic Career Process is a journey designed to provide you with the personal insight and skills necessary to make your career part of your spiritual path.

The sequence you have followed throughout this process is based on personal insights as well as professional realities to address the spiritual anorexia that keeps us focused on short-term commercial gain regardless of the cost. Evidence of the longing in the hearts of individuals throughout our culture to find a deeper meaning and purpose in their work, to understand the mysteries of life and the human spirit, and to reconnect with the power of nature is shown by the explosion in books on spirituality and mysticism that has taken place over the past several years. However, the ability to integrate the wisdom of many of these authors and inspirational speakers into our daily lives often remains elusive. People who leave motivational retreats genuinely inspired frequently report that, without a plan for using the insights they have gleaned to deal with the level of daily stress and mental fragmentation they endure on the job, their feelings of resentment and futility quickly return.

To be relevant to you and your career, this work is designed to help you get in touch with practical spirituality. It takes persistence and commitment to integrate the skills and insights you have developed throughout this process into your daily life. You may find it helpful to consider the following suggestions in order to use the Authentic Career Process as a framework for your ongoing evolution:

- *Repeating an exercise increases its power.* Pick an exercise that was particularly meaningful for you, and repeat this work as you continue to evolve. You will experience the benefits of the same exercise at deeper levels as you connect more fully with your authentic self.

- *Practice patience.* If you found yourself rushing through any of the exercises your first time through, go back and try them again. Be mindful of any messages your body sends you, and try to stick with these exercises, even if you do not experience immediate results. Often, we will unconsciously rush through or trivialize work that can unlock powerful realizations for us because some part of our being is anxious about this facet of self-discovery.

- *Connect this process to your everyday life.* Identify an exercise that was particularly helpful to you, and reflect on its meaning in your daily life. The power in this work comes from its ability to influence our daily habits of thought and action.

- *Remember your boundaries.* Sharing your insights prematurely with people who may not understand them often dissipates the positive energy you are building. This work is about an internal evolution that helps you take back your personal power in a world that encourages us to gain much of our esteem through the approval of others. Be mindful of whether the people you share your dreams and desires with are supportive of your authentic growth.

- *Pace yourself, and be gentle with yourself.* Remember that trying too hard is a form of resistance. There is a danger in moving so fast that you don't have time to anchor your new insights and skills in your daily life. Rushing will create a backlash that may leave you feeling frustrated and disillusioned. Keep checking in with yourself about the pace that is right for you.

- *Reread your previous work.* One of the most meaningful aspects of writing in a journal is going back and reading what you have written to yourself at a previous time. It takes time for new

Once in a while you get shown the light in the strangest of places if you look right at it.

— Robert Hunter

insights and goals to incubate in the less-conscious parts of our being. Rereading what you have written about your discoveries and desires can be a powerful catalyst for keeping your energy focused on achieving your authentic desires.

Every desire you have, every craving you feel, and every pang of insecurity or even jealousy you experience is a sacred part of your authentic self. The Authentic Career Process is aimed at helping you remember how every competing energy within you is actually integrated at the core of your being. When you learn to accept yourself in your totality, you will discover a sense of personal power that can be focused to achieve almost anything. What's more, when you learn to accept yourself you will find that you automatically accept others. This dynamic obviously has widespread implications for our culture and our world. Thus, when you are sincerely engaged in making the most of your own resources both personally and professionally, you are automatically contributing to others in the deepest possible sense. As we rebuild ourselves, we rebuild our world.

Take the first step in faith. You don't have to see the whole staircase, just to take the first step.
— Martin Luther King, Jr.

I have experienced both a public and a private evolution. My professional evolution has been pretty easy to describe publicly. Many people have told me they can easily relate to my professional experiences. After all, since I have been fortunate enough to have enjoyed some modest trappings of success as our culture defines it, hearing this part of my evolution doesn't take people too far out of their comfort zones.

However, my spiritual evolution has been a different matter. The moments of grace that have shaped my understanding of spirituality and how it applies to authentic success have been "energetic experiences" that I can't always find words to describe.

What's more, dealing with the topic of spiritual growth often makes many people in the business world distinctly uncomfortable. Senior executives driven to focus on monetary gain (particularly personal gain) often prefer to think of spirituality as a sentimental concept that can be neatly compartmentalized into their private time.

They will pooh-pooh the importance of spiritual principles in business by claiming that they are too "touchy-feely" to have a meaningful impact on profitability. This is the mind-set of executives who also tend to ignore warnings about dwindling morale, corruption, and poor communication.

I have been driven to write this book because of my knowledge that learning to cultivate our spiritual resources is vital both to individuals who want to create meaningful careers and organizations that want to create enduring value. Therefore, I will continue to stress the importance of spiritual resources, in spite of the risk of being dismissed by some pretty powerful naysayers.

Authentic spiritual growth is about going within to find your answers, not looking anxiously to others to define you. What is most important is getting in alignment with you and no one else. In other words, feel free to honor your own healthy skepticism. You should never take anyone else's word for spiritual truth. Spiritual truth is knowledge born of personal experience.

One of the great leaders of history was Napoleon Bonaparte. Napoleon was an avid student of spiritual principles and a masterful leader of men. He once fondled a velvet curtain in his chamber and told those close to him, "I could make a man die for this." What made this petite general so confident of this chilling fact?

Napoleon understood that many of us operate, much more than we believe, from an infantile sense of danger. Many of us have been trained, since infancy, to look anxiously to those in power for approval, security, and validation. Terrified of the level of self-knowledge required to take full responsibility for our own lives, many of us have learned to literally worship those in power who we believe will protect us from the crushing burden of facing our fears and thinking for ourselves. Napoleon knew that many people, driven by a childlike need to please those in power, would literally die for that curtain if it were designated as the latest symbol of achievement or prestige.

I've tried to "die for that curtain" many times in my own life, and

I am free to be what I want to be and to do what I want to do.

— Richard Bach

every time my Higher Power has saved me before I was stupid enough to fall on my sword. I've tried eagerly to give my power away to prestigious corporate hierarchies, exciting lovers, and even intellectually seductive therapists and spiritual leaders who seemed qualified to lead me when I was too tired to lead myself. However, every time I've looked outside myself to find the answers I needed, the sacred lesson I've learned is that I was looking in the wrong place.

The foundation of authentic personal power is trust. We build this foundation by learning to trust ourselves — at all levels of consciousness. When our foundation of self-trust is solid, we find that we will be able to trust and work productively with others, because we will have honed our instincts in selecting the right relationships and the right environment to help us achieve our goals.

Throughout the Authentic Career Process, I've tried to give you a variety of tools to enhance your self-awareness and build your skills. As you apply these tools to your career and your life, remember that everything you need to achieve your dreams is already inside you — absolutely everything.

When you realize your own authentic potential, you are playing a vital part in the timeless cycle of human evolution. Never forget that while your career is one of your most precious possessions, it is also your greatest gift to others.

Thank you for allowing my work to be part of your journey. I wish you the best of success.

There are two ways to live your life.
One is as though nothing is a miracle.
The other is as though everything is a miracle.

— Albert Einstein

Index

Maggie Craddock has worked as an executive coach with clients across the professional spectrum — from freelance professionals to brand-new corporate vice presidents and Fortune 500 CEOs. She has been featured on CNBC and National Public Radio and quoted in such publications as the *Wall Street Journal*, the *Los Angeles Times*, and the *Chicago Tribune*. Maggie is the author of several syndicated articles on behavioral dynamics in the workplace, and her work has been featured in *O: The Oprah Magazine*. She speaks throughout the world on workplace issues, with audiences ranging from regular leadership conferences for her corporate clients, the graduating classes of Harvard and Columbia business schools, and Deutsche Bank's annual Women on Wall Street conference.

About the Author

Before becoming an executive coach, Maggie worked for over a decade on both the buy side and the sell side of the financial services industry. As a portfolio manager at Scudder, Stevens & Clark, Maggie managed $3 billion in short-term global assets. During her time on Wall Street, she received two Lipper Awards for top mutual fund performance.

Maggie received a M.Sc. in Economics from the London School of Economics, specializing in Capital Markets. She also received an M.S.W. from New York University and is an Ackerman certified family therapist. Maggie also holds a B.A. in Economics from Smith College and serves on the Women's Leadership Board for the Kennedy School of Government at Harvard University. Her website, www.workplacerelationships.com, provides an overview of her coaching methodology.

In her spare time, Maggie pursues her passionate interest in visiting the great trees of the world. She has gone across the country to learn about, photograph, and sketch trees in national forests, botanical gardens, and along nature trails. She lives in New York City.

New World Library is dedicated to
publishing books and audio products
that inspire and challenge us to improve
the quality of our lives and our world.

Our products are available
in bookstores everywhere.
For our catalog, please contact:

New World Library
14 Pamaron Way
Novato, California 94949

Phone: (415) 884-2100 or (800) 972-6657
Catalog requests: Ext. 50
Orders: Ext. 52
Fax: (415) 884-2199

Email: escort@newworldlibrary.com
Website: www.newworldlibrary.com